Cross-Language Knowledge Induction Workshop 2006

Held at EACL 2006

Trento, Italy
3 April 2006

ISBN: 978-1-61738-485-1

Printed from e-media with permission by:

Curran Associates, Inc.
57 Morehouse Lane
Red Hook, NY 12571
www.proceedings.com

Some format issues inherent in the e-media version may also appear in this print version.

Printed by Curran Associates, Inc. (2010)

Association for Computational Linguistics
209 N. Eighth Street
Stroudsburg, Pennsylvania 18360

Phone: 1-570-476-8006
Fax: 1-570-476-0860

acl@aclweb.org

Preface

Knowledge of the behavior of words and text in other languages has recently been used to help solving tasks in a first language. An example of such a task is word-sense disambiguation by using translations in a second language. Another example is verb classification by studying properties of verbs in several languages.

A second modality of knowledge transfer across languages is to take advantage of resources already built for English and for a few other resource-rich languages. These resources have been used to induce knowledge in languages for which few linguistic resources are available. This was made possible by the wider availability of parallel corpora and better alignment methods at paragraph, sentence, and word level. Examples of such knowledge induction tasks are learning morphology, part-of-speech tags and grammatical gender. Cross-language knowledge transfer has also been possible thanks to the development of wordnets aligned to the original Princeton WordNet.

This workshop provides a forum for discussion between leading names and researchers involved in cross-language applications. Topics of interest include, but are not limited to: applications that exploit parallel corpora (learning morphological segmentation; learning part-of-speech; learning grammatical gender; other applications); induction of knowledge from a language for which resources are abundant to another language for which fewer resources are available; using other languages to solve a task in a first language (word-sense disambiguation by using translations in other languages; verb classification by studying verb properties in several languages; other tasks of this kind); identifying and using cognate words between languages; building wordnets by knowledge transfer; and exploiting multi-language wordnets for NLP applications.

We would like to thank all the authors who submitted papers for the hard work that went behind their submissions. We express our deepest gratitude to the committee members for their thorough reviews. We also thank the EACL 2006 organizers for their help with administrative matters.

Diana Inkpen
Carlo Strapparava
Eneko Agirre

Organizing committee

Diana Inkpen (University of Ottawa, Canada)
Carlo Strapparava (ITC-IRST, Povo-Trento, Italy)
Eneko Agirre (University of the Basque Country, Donostia, Spain)

Program Committee

Paul Buitelaar (DFKI, Saarbrucken, Germany)
Silviu Cucerzan (Microsoft Research, US)
Mona Diab (Columbia University, US)
Greg Kondrak (University of Alberta, Canada)
Lluís Màrquez (Universitat Politècnica de Catalunya, Barcelona, Spain)
Joel Martin (National Research Council of Canada)
Rada Mihalcea (University of North Texas, US)
Viviana Nastase (University of Ottawa, Canada)
Ted Pedersen (University of Minnesota, Duluth, US)
Emanuele Pianta (ITC-IRST, Povo-Trento, Italy)
Philip Resnik (University of Maryland, US)
German Rigau (University of the Basque Country, Donostia, Spain)
Laurent Romary (LORIA, Nancy, France)
Michel Simard (National Research Council of Canada)
Suzanne Stevenson (University of Toronto, Canada)
Doina Tatar (Babes-Bolyai University, Cluj-Napoca, Romania)
Amalia Todirascu (Université Marc Bloch, Strasbourg, France)
Dan Tufis (Romanian Academy, Bucharest, Romania)
Nikolai Vazov (University of Sofia, Bulgaria)

Invited Speakers

Mona Diab (Columbia University, US)
Dan Tufis (Romanian Academy, Bucharest, Romania)

Workshop Program

8:50 – 9:00	*Welcome and Introduction*
9:00 – 10:00	*Invited talk*: Mona Diab
10:00 – 10:30	*Multilingual Extension of a Temporal Expression Normalizer using Annotated Corpora* E. Saquete, P. Martínez-Barco, R. Muñoz, M. Negri, M. Speranza and R. Sprugnoli
10:30 – 11:00	Break
11:00 – 11:30	*A Framework for Incorporating Alignment Information in Parsing* Mark Hopkins and Jonas Kuhn
11:30 – 12:00	*Induction of Cross-Language Affix and Letter Sequence Correspondence* Ari Rappoport and Tsahi Levent-Levi
12:00 – 12:30	*Improving Name Discrimination: A Language Salad Approach* Ted Pedersen, Anagha Kulkarni, Roxana Angheluta, Zornitsa Kozareva, and Thamar Solorio
12:30 – 14:30	Lunch
14:30 – 15:30	*Invited talk*: Dan Tufis
15:30 – 16:00	*Tagging Portuguese with a Spanish Tagger* Jirka Hana, Anna Feldman, Luiz Amaral, and Chris Brew
16:00 – 16:30	Break
16:30 – 17:00	*Automatic Generation of Translation Dictionaries Using Intermediary Languages* Kisuh Ahn and Matthew Frampton
17:00 – 17:30	*Word Sense Disambiguation Using Automatically Translated Sense Examples* Xinglong Wang and David Martinez
17:30 – 18:00	*Projecting POS Tags and Syntactic Dependencies from English and French to Polish in Aligned Corpora* Sylwia Ozdowska

Table of Contents

Multilingual Extension of a Temporal Expression Normalizer using Annotated Corpora
E. Saquete, P. Martnez-Barco, R. Muoz, M. Negri, M. Speranza and R. Sprugnoli 1

A Framework for Incorporating Alignment Information in Parsing
Mark Hopkins and Jonas Kuhn 9

induction of cross-language affix and letter sequence correspondence
Ari Rappoport and Tsahi Levent-Levi 17

Improving Name Discrimination: A Language Salad Approach
Ted Pedersen, Anagha Kulkarni, Roxana Angheluta, Zornitsa Kozareva and Thamar Solorio 25

Tagging Portuguese with a Spanish Tagger
Jirka Hana, Anna Feldman, Luiz Amaral and Chris Brew 33

Automatic Generation of Translation Dictionaries Using Intermediary Languages
Kisuh Ahn and Matthew Frampton 41

Word Sense Disambiguation Using Automatically Translated Sense Examples
Xinglong Wang and David Martinez 45

Projecting POS tags and syntactic dependencies from English and French to Polish in aligned corpora
Sylwia Ozdowska 53

The conference, the workshop and the tutorials are sponsored by:

Center for the Evaluation of Language and Communication Technologies

Celct
c/o BIC, Via dei Solteri, 38
38100 Trento, Italy
http://www.celct.it

Xerox Research Centre Europe
6 Chemin de Maupertuis
38240 Meylan, France
http://www.xrce.xerox.com

CELI s.r.l.
Corso Moncalieri, 21
10131 Torino, Italy
http://www.celi.it

Thales
45 rue de Villiers
92526 Neuilly-sur-Seine Cedex, France
http://www.thalesgroup.com

EACL-2006 is supported by

Trentino S.p.a. and Metalsistem Group

Multilingual Extension of a Temporal Expression Normalizer using Annotated Corpora

E. Saquete P. Martínez-Barco R. Muñoz
gPLSI
DLSI. UA
Alicante, Spain
{stela,patricio,rafael}@dlsi.ua.es

M. Negri M. Speranza
ITC-irst
Povo (TN), Italy
{negri,manspera}@itc.it

R. Sprugnoli
CELCT
Trento, Italy
sprugnoli@celct.it

Abstract

This paper presents the automatic extension to other languages of TERSEO, a knowledge-based system for the recognition and normalization of temporal expressions originally developed for Spanish[1]. TERSEO was first extended to English through the automatic translation of the temporal expressions. Then, an improved porting process was applied to Italian, where the automatic translation of the temporal expressions from English and from Spanish was combined with the extraction of new expressions from an Italian annotated corpus. Experimental results demonstrate how, while still adhering to the rule-based paradigm, the development of automatic rule translation procedures allowed us to minimize the effort required for porting to new languages. Relying on such procedures, and without any manual effort or previous knowledge of the target language, TERSEO recognizes and normalizes temporal expressions in Italian with good results (72% precision and 83% recall for recognition).

1 Introduction

Recently, the Natural Language Processing community has become more and more interested in developing language independent systems, in the effort of breaking the language barrier hampering their application in real use scenarios. Such a strong interest in multilinguality is demonstrated by the growing number of international conferences and initiatives placing systems' multilingual/cross-language capabilities among the hottest research topics, such as the European Cross-Language Evaluation Forum[2] (CLEF), a successful evaluation campaign which aims at fostering research in different areas of multilingual information retrieval. At the same time, in the temporal expressions recognition and normalization field, systems featuring multilingual capabilities have been proposed. Among others, (Moia, 2001; Wilson et al., 2001; Negri and Marseglia, 2004) emphasized the potentialities of such applications for different information retrieval related tasks.

As many other NLP areas, research in automated temporal reasoning has recently seen the emergence of machine learning approaches trying to overcome the difficulties of extending a language model to other languages (Carpenter, 2004; Ittycheriah et al., 2003). In this direction, the outcomes of the first Time Expression Recognition and Normalization Workshop (TERN 2004[3]) provide a clear indication of the state of the field. In spite of the good results obtained in the *recognition* task, *normalization* by means of machine learning techniques still shows relatively poor results with respect to rule-based approaches, and still remains an unresolved problem.

The difficulty of porting systems to new languages (or domains) affects both rule-based and machine learning approaches. With rule-based approaches (Schilder and Habel, 2001; Filatova and Hovy, 2001), the main problems are related to the fact that the porting process requires rewriting from scratch, or adapting to each new language, large numbers of rules, which is costly and time-

[1] This research was partially funded by the Spanish Government (contract TIC2003-07158-C04-01)

[2] http://www.clef-campaign.org/

[3] http://timex2.mitre.org/tern.html

consuming work. Machine learning approaches (Setzer and Gaizauskas, 2002; Katz and Arosio, 2001), on the other hand, can be extended with little human intervention through the use of language corpora. However, the large annotated corpora that are necessary to obtain high performance are not always available. In this paper we describe a new procedure to build temporal models for new languages, starting from previously defined ones. While still adhering to the rule-based paradigm, its main contribution is the proposal of a simple, but effective, methodology to automate the porting of a system from one language to another. In this procedure, we take advantage of the architecture of an existing system developed for Spanish (TERSEO, see (Saquete et al., 2005)), where the recognition model is language-dependent but the normalizing procedure is completely independent. In this way, the approach is capable of automatically learning the recognition model by adjusting the set of normalization rules.

The paper is structured as follows: Section 2 provides a short overview of TERSEO; Section 3 describes the automatic extension of the system to Italian; Section 4 presents the results of our evaluation experiments, comparing the performance of Ita-TERSEO (i.e. our extended system) with the performance of a state of the art system for Italian.

2 The TERSEO system architecture

TERSEO has been developed in order to automatically recognize temporal expressions (TEs) appearing in a Spanish written text, and normalize them according to the temporal model proposed in (Saquete, 2005), which is compatible with the ACE annotation standards for temporal expressions (Ferro et al., 2005). As shown in Figure 1, the first step (recognition) includes pre-processing of the input texts, which are tagged with lexical and morphological information that will be used as input to the temporal parser. The temporal parser is implemented using an ascending technique (chart parser) and is based on a temporal grammar. Once the parser has recognized the TEs in an input text, these are passed to the normalization unit, which updates the value of the reference according to the date they refer to, and generates the XML tags for each expression.

As TEs can be categorized as explicit and implicit, the grammar used by the parser is tuned for discriminating between the two groups. On the

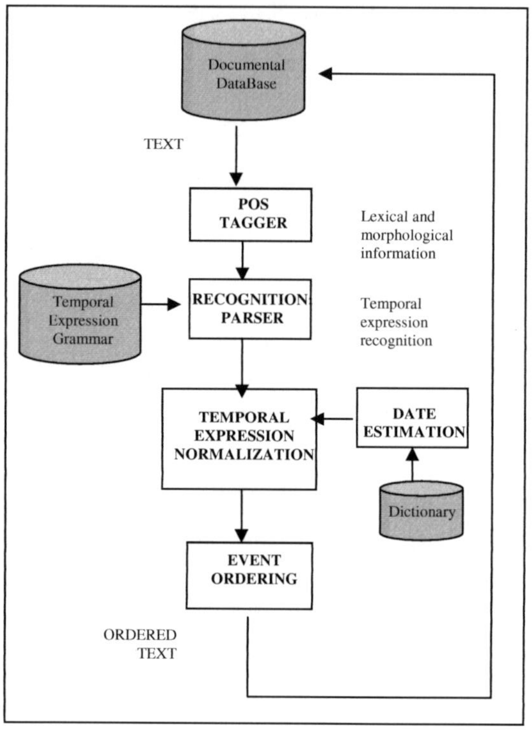

Figure 1: Graphic representation of the TERSEO architecture.

one hand, *explicit* temporal expressions directly provide and fully describe a date which does not require any further reasoning process to be interpreted (e.g. "1st May 2005", "05/01/2005"). On the other hand, *implicit* (or anaphoric) time expressions (e.g. "yesterday", "three years later") require some degree of reasoning (as in the case of anaphora resolution). In order to translate such expressions into explicit dates, such reasoning capabilities consider the information provided by the lexical context in which they occur (see (Saquete, 2005) for a thorough description of the reasoning techniques used by TERSEO).

2.1 Recognition using a temporal expression parser

The parser uses a grammar based on two different sets of rules. The first set of rules is in charge of date and time recognition (i.e. explicit dates, such as "05/01/2005"). For this type of TEs, the grammar adopted by TERSEO recognizes a large number of date and time formats (see Table 1 for some examples).

The second set of rules is in charge of the recognition of the temporal reference for implicit TEs,

`fecha→ dd+'/'+mm+'/'+(yy)yy`	(12/06/1975) *(06/12/1975)*
`fecha→ dd+'-'+mes+'-'+(yy)yy`	(12-junio-1975) *(12-Jun.-1975)*
`fecha→ dd+'de'+mm+'de'+(yy)yy`	(12 de junio de 1975)

Table 1: Sample of rules for Explicit Dates Recognition.

Implicit dates referring to Document Date Concrete	`reference→ 'ayer'`	*(yesterday)*
	`reference→ 'mañana'`	*(tomorrow)*
	`reference→ 'anteayer'`	*(the day before yesterdary)*
	`reference→ 'el próximo día'`	*(the next day)*
Implicit Dates Previous Date Period	`reference→ 'un mes después'`	*(a month later)*
	`reference→ num+'años después'`	*(num years later)*
Imp. Dates Prev.Date Concrete	`reference→ 'un día antes'`	*(a day before)*
Implicit Dates Previous Date Fuzzy	`reference→ 'días después'`	*(some days later)*
	`reference→ 'días antes'`	*(some days before)*

Table 2: Sample of rules for Implicit Dates recognition.

i.e. TEs that need to be related to an explicit TE to be interpreted. These can be divided into time adverbs (e.g. "yesterday", "tomorrow"), and nominal phrases that are referring to temporal relationships (e.g. "three years later", "the day before"). Table 2 shows some of the rules used for the detection of these kinds of references.

2.2 Normalization

When the system finds an explicit temporal expression, the normalization process is direct as no resolution of the expression is necessary. For implicit expressions, an inference engine that interprets every reference previously found in the input text is used. In some cases references are solved using the newspaper's date (FechaP). Other TEs have to be interpreted by referring to a date named before in the text that is being analyzed (FechaA). In these cases, a temporal model that allows the system to determine the reference date over which the dictionary operations are going to be done, has been defined. This model is based on the following two rules:

1. The newspaper's date, when available, is used as a base temporal referent by default; otherwise, the current date is used as anchor.

2. In case a non-anaphoric TE is found, it is stored as FechaA. This value is updated every time a non-anaphoric TE appears in the text.

Table 3 shows some of the entries of the dictionary used in the inference engine.

3 Extending TERSEO: from Spanish and English to Italian

As stated before, the main purpose of this paper is to describe a new procedure to automatically build temporal models for new languages, starting from previously defined models. In our case, an English model has been automatically obtained from the Spanish one through the automatic translation of the Spanish temporal expressions to English. The resulting system for the recognition and normalization of English TEs obtains good results both in terms of precision (P) and recall (R) (Saquete et al., 2004). The comparison of the results between the Spanish and the English system is shown in Table 4.

	SPANISH	ENGLISH
DOCS	50	100
POS	199	634
ACT	156	511
CORRECT	138	393
INCORRECT	18	118
MISSED	43	123
P	88%	77%
R	69%	62%
F	77%	69%

Table 4: Comparison between Spanish TERSEO and English TERSEO.

This section presents the procedure we followed to extend our system to Italian, starting from the Spanish and English models already available, and a manually annotated corpus. In this case, both models have been considered as they can be complemented reciprocally. The Spanish model was

REFERENCE	DICTIONARY ENTRY
'ayer' *(yesterday)*	Day(FechaP)-1/Month(FechaP)/Year(FechaP)
'mañana' (tomorrow)	Day(FechaP)+1/Month(FechaP)/Year(FechaP)
'anteayer' *(the day before yesterday)*	Day(FechaP)-2/Month(FechaP)/Year(FechaP)
'el próximo día' *(the next day)*	Day(FechaP)+1/Month(FechaP)/Year(FechaP)
'un mes después' *(a month later)*	[DayI/Month(FechaA)+1/Year(FechaA)-- DayF/Month(FechaA)+1/Year(FechaA)]
num+'años después' *(num years later)*	[01/01/Year(FechaA)+num -- 31/12/Year(FechaA)+num]
'un día antes' *(a day before)*	Day(FechaA)-1/Month(FechaA)/Year(FechaA)
'días después' *(some days later)*	>>>>FechaA
'días antes' *(some days before)*	<<<<FechaA

Table 3: Normalization rules

manually obtained and evaluated showing high scores for precision (88%), so better results could be expected when it is used. However, in spite of the fact that the English model has shown lower results on precision (77%), the on-line translators between Italian and English have better results than Spanish to Italian translators. As a result, both models are considered in the following steps for the multilingual extension:

- Firstly, a set of Italian temporal expressions is extracted from an Italian annotated corpus and stored in a database. The selected corpus is the training part of I-CAB, the Italian Content Annotation Bank (Lavelli et al., 2005). More detailed information about I-CAB is provided in Section 4.

- Secondly, the resulting set of Italian TEs must be related to the appropriate normalization rule. In order to do that, a double translation procedure has been developed. We first translate all the expressions into English and Spanish simultaneously; then, the normalization rules related to the translated expressions are obtained. If both the Spanish and English expressions are found in their respective models in agreement with the same normalization rule, then this rule is also assigned to the Italian expression. Also, when only one of the translated expressions is found in the existing models, the normalization rule is assigned. In case of discrepancies, i.e. if both expressions are found, but not coinciding in the same normalization rule, then one of the languages must be prioritized. As the Spanish model was manually obtained and has shown a higher precision, Spanish rules are preferred. In other cases, the expression is reserved for a manual assignment.

- Finally, the set is automatically augmented using the Spanish and English sets of temporal expressions. These expressions were also translated into Italian by on-line machine translation systems (Spanish-Italian[4], English-Italian[5]). In this case, a filtering module is used to guarantee that all the expressions were correctly translated. This module searches the web with Google[6] for the translated expression. If the expression is not frequently found, then the translation is abandoned. After that, the new Italian expression is included in the model, and related to the same normalization rule assigned to the Spanish or English temporal expression.

The entire translation process has been completed with an automatic generalization process, oriented to obtain generalized rules from the concrete cases that have been collected from the cor-

[4]http://www.tranexp.com:2000/Translate/result.shtml
[5]http://world.altavista.com/
[6]http://www.google.com/

pus. This generalization process has a double effect. On the one hand, it reduces the number of recognition rules. On the other hand, it allows the system to identify new expressions that were not previously learned. For instance, the expression *"Dieci mesi dopo"* (i.e. "Ten months later") could be recognized if the expression *"Nove mesi dopo"* (i.e. Nine months later) was learned.

The multilingual extension procedure (Figure 3) is carried out in three phases:

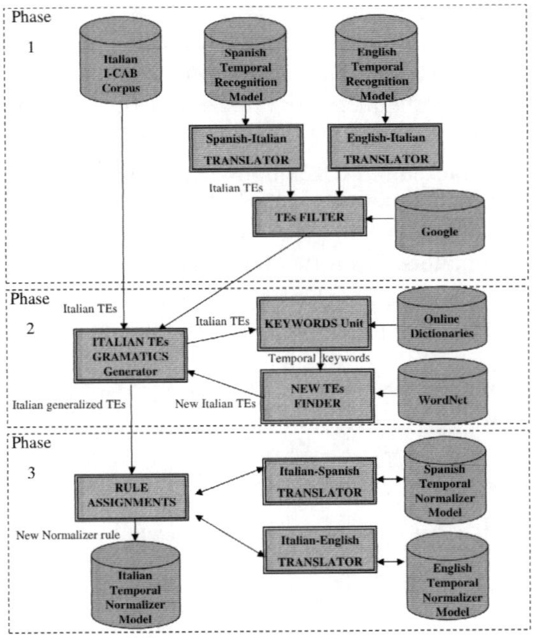

Figure 2: Multilingual extension procedure.

- Phase 1: TE Collection. During this phase, the Italian temporal expressions are collected from I-CAB (Italian Content Annotation Bank), and the automatically translated Italian TEs are derived from the set of Spanish and English TEs. In this case, the TEs are filtered removing those not being found by Google.

- Phase 2: TE Generalization. In this phase, the TEs Gramatics Generator uses the morphological and syntactical information from the collected TEs to generate the grammatical rules that generalize the recognition of the TEs. Moreover, the keyword unit is able to extract the temporal keywords that will be used to build new TEs. These keywords are augmented with their synonyms in WordNet (Vossen, 2000) to generate new TEs.

- Phase 3: TE Normalizing Rule Assignment. In the last phase, the translators are used to relate the recognizing rule to the appropriate normalization rule. For this purpose, the system takes advantage of the previously defined Spanish and English temporal models.

4 Evaluation

The automatic extension of the system to Italian (Ita-TERSEO) has been evaluated using I-CAB, which has been divided in two parts: training and test. The training part has been used, first of all, in order to automatically extend the system. After this extension, the system was evaluated both against the training and the test corpora. The purpose of this double evaluation experiment was to compare the recall obtained over the training corpus with the value obtained over the test corpus.

An additional evaluation experiment has also been carried out in order to compare the performance of the automatically developed system with a state of the art system specifically developed for Italian and English, i.e. the Chronos system described in (Negri and Marseglia, 2004).

In the following sections, more details about I-CAB and the evaluation process are presented, together with the evaluation results.

4.1 The I-CAB Corpus

The evaluation has been performed on the temporal annotations of I-CAB (I-CAB-temp) created as part of the three-year project ONTOTEXT[7] funded by the Provincia Autonoma di Trento.

I-CAB consists of 525 news documents taken from the local newspaper L'Adige (http://www.adige.it). The selected news stories belong to four different days (September, 7th and 8th 2004 and October, 7th and 8th 2004) and are grouped into five categories: News Stories, Cultural News, Economic News, Sports News and Local News. The corpus consists of around 182,500 words (on average 347 words per file). The total number of annotated temporal expressions is 4,553; the average length of a temporal expression is 1.9 words.

The annotation of I-CAB has been carried out adopting the standards developed within the ACE program (Automatic Content Extraction[8]) for the Time Expressions Recognition and Normalization

[7] http://tcc.itc.it/projects/ontotext

[8] http://www.nist.gov/speech/tests/ace

tasks, which allows for a semantically rich and normalized annotation of different types of temporal expressions (for further details on the TIMEX2 annotation standard for English see (Ferro et al., 2005)).

The ACE guidelines have been adapted to the specific morpho-syntactic features of Italian, which has a far richer morphology than English. In particular, some changes concerning the extension of the temporal expressions have been introduced. According to the English guidelines, in fact, definite and indefinite articles are considered as part of the textual realization of an entity, while prepositions are not. As the annotation is word-based, this does not account for Italian articulated prepositions, where a definite article and a preposition are merged. Within I-CAB, this type of preposition has been included as possible constituents of an entity, so as to consistently include all the articles.

An assessment of the inter-annotator agreement based on the Dice coefficient has shown that the task is a well-defined one, as the agreement is 95.5% for the recognition of temporal expressions.

4.2 Evaluation process

The evaluation of the automatic extension of TERSEO to Italian has been performed in three steps. First of all, the system has been evaluated both against the training and the test corpora with two main purposes:

- Determining if the recall obtained in the evaluation of the training part of the corpus is a bit higher than the one obtained in the evaluation of the test part of I-CAB, due to the fact that in the TE collection phase of the extension, temporal expressions were extracted from this part of the corpus.
- Determining the performance of the automatically extended system without any manual revision of both the Italian translations and the resolution rules automatically related to the expressions.

Secondly, we were also interested in verifying if the performance of the system in terms of precision could be improved through a manual revision of the automatically translated temporal expressions.

Finally, a comparison with a state of the art system for Italian has been carried out in order to estimate the real potentialities of the proposed approach. All the evaluation results are compared and presented in the following sections using the same metrics adopted at the TERN2004 conference.

4.2.1 Evaluation of Ita-TERSEO

In the automatic extension of the system, a total of 1,183 Italian temporal expressions have been stored in the database. As shown in Table 5, these expressions have been obtained from the different resources available:

- ENG_ITA: This group of expressions has been obtained from the automatic translation into Italian of the English Temporal Expressions stored in the knowledge DB.
- ESP_ITA: This group of expressions has been obtained from the automatic translation into Italian of the Spanish Temporal Expressions stored in the knowledge DB.
- CORPUS: This group of expressions has been extracted directly from the training part of the I-CAB corpus.

Source	N	%
ENG_ITA	593	50.1
ESP_ITA	358	30.3
CORPUS	232	19.6
TOTAL TEs	1183	100.0

Table 5: Italian TEs in the Knowledge DB.

Both the training part and the test part of I-CAB have been used for evaluation. The results of precision (P), recall (R) and F-Measure (F) are presented in Table 6, which provides details about the system performance over the general recognition task (timex2), and the different normalization attributes used by the TIMEX2 annotation standard.

As expected, recall performance over the training corpus is slightly higher. However, although the temporal expressions have been extracted from such corpus, in the automatic process of obtaining the normalization rules for these expressions, some errors could have been introduced.

Comparing these results with those obtained by the automatic extension of TERSEO to English and taking into account the recognition task (see Table 4), precision (P) is slightly better for English (77% Vs. 72%) whereas recall (R) is better in the Italian extension (62% Vs. 83%). This is

Tag	Ita-TERSEO: TRAINING P	R	F	Ita-TERSEO: TEST P	R	F	Chronos: TEST P	R	F
timex2	0.694	0.848	0.763	0.726	0.834	0.776	0.925	0.908	0.917
anchor_dir	0.495	0.562	0.526	0.578	0.475	0.521	0.733	0.636	0.681
anchor_val	0.464	0.527	0.493	0.516	0.424	0.465	0.495	0.462	0.478
set	0.308	0.903	0.459	0.182	1.000	0.308	0.616	0.5	0.552
text	0.265	0.324	0.292	0.258	0.296	0.276	0.859	0.843	0.851
val	0.581	0.564	0.573	0.564	0.545	0.555	0.636	0.673	0.654

Table 6: Results obtained over I-CAB by Ita-TERSEO and Chronos.

due to the fact that in the Italian extension, more temporal expressions have been covered with respect to the English extension. In this case, in fact, Ita-TERSEO is not only using the temporal expressions translated from the English or Spanish knowledge database, but also the temporal expressions extracted from the training part of I-CAB.

4.2.2 Manual revision of the acquired TEs

A manual revision of the Italian TEs stored in the Knowledge DB has been done in two steps. First of all, the incorrectly translated expressions (from Spanish and English to Italian) were removed from the database. A total of 334 expressions were detected as wrong translated expressions. After this, another revision was performed. In this case, some expressions were modified because the expressions have some minor errors in the translation. 213 expressions were modified in this second revision cycle. Moreover, since pattern constituents in Italian might have different orthographical features (e.g. masculine/feminine, initial vowel/consonant, etc.), new patterns had to be introduced to capture such variants. For example, as months' names in Italian could start with a vowel, the temporal expression pattern "nell'-MONTH" has been inserted in the Knowledge DB. After these changes, the total amount of expressions stored in the DB are shown in Table 7.

Source	N	%
ING_ITA	416	47.9
ESP_ITA	201	23.1
CORPUS	232	26.7
REV_MAN	20	2.3
TOTAL TEs	869	100.0

Table 7: Italian TEs in the Knowledge DB after manual revision.

In order to evaluate the system after this manual revision, the training and the test part of I-CAB have been used. However, the results of precision (PREC), recall (REC) and F-Measure were exactly the same as presented in Table 6. That is not really surprising. The existence of wrong expressions in the knowledge database does not affect the final results of the system, as they will never be used for recognition or resolution. This is because these expressions will not appear in real documents, and are redundant as the correct expression is also stored in the Knowledge DB.

4.2.3 Comparing Italian TERSEO with a language-specific system

Finally, in order to compare Ita-TERSEO with a state of the art system specifically designed for Italian, we chose Chronos (Negri and Marseglia, 2004), a multilingual system for the recognition and normalization of TEs in Italian and English. Like all the other state of the art systems addressing the recognition/normalization task, Chronos is a rule-based system. From a design point of view, it shares with TERSEO a rather similar architecture which relies on different sets of rules. These are regular expressions that check for specific features of the input text, such as the presence of particular word senses, lemmas, parts of speech, symbols, or strings satisfying specific predicates. Each set of rules is in charge of dealing with different aspects of the problem. In particular, a set of around 350 rules is designed for TE recognition and is capable of recognizing with high Precision/Recall rates both explicit and implicit TEs. Other sets of regular expressions, for a total of around 700 rules, are used in the normalization phase, and are in charge of handling a specific TIMEX2 attribute (i.e. VAL, SET, ANCHOR_VAL, and ANCHOR_DIR). The results obtained by the Italian version of Chronos over the test part of I-CAB are shown in the last three columns of Table 6.

As expected, the distance between the results obtained by the two systems is considerable. However, the following considerations should be taken into account. First, there is a great difference, both in terms of the required time and effort, in the development of the two systems. While the implementation of the manual one took several months, the porting procedure of TERSEO to Italian is a very fast process that can be accomplished in less than an hour. Second, even if an annotated corpus for a new language is not available, the automatic porting procedure we present still remains feasible. In fact, most of the TEs for a new language that are stored in the Knowledge DB are the result of the translation of the Spanish/English TEs into such a target language. In our case, as shown in Table 5, more than 80% of the acquired Italian TEs result from the automatic translation of the expressions already stored in the DB. This makes the proposed approach a viable solution which allows for a rapid porting of the system to other languages, while just requiring an on-line translator (note that the Altavista Babel Fish translator[9] provides translations from English to 12 target languages). In light of these considerations, the results obtained by Ita-TERSEO are encouraging.

5 Conclusions

In this paper we have presented an automatic extension of a rule-based approach to TEs recognition and normalization. The procedure is based on building temporal models for new languages starting from previously defined ones. This procedure is able to fill the gap left by machine learning systems that, up to date, are still far from providing acceptable performance on this task. As results illustrate, the proposed methodology (even though with a lower performance with respect to language-specific systems) is a viable and effective solution for a rapid and automatic porting of an existing system to new languages.

References

B. Carpenter. 2004. Phrasal Queries with LingPipe and Lucene. In *13th Text REtrieval Conference*, NIST Special Publication. National Institute of Standards and Technology.

L. Ferro, L. Gerber, I. Mani, B. Sundheim, and G. Wilson. 2005. TIDES 2005 Standard for the annotation of temporal expressions. Technical report, MITRE.

E. Filatova and E. Hovy. 2001. Assigning time-stamps to event-clauses. In ACL, editor, *Proceedings of the 2001 ACL Workshop on Temporal and Spatial Information Processing*, pages 88–95, Toulouse, France.

[9]http://world.altavista.com/

A. Ittycheriah, L.V. Lita, N. Kambhatla, N. Nicolov, S. Roukos, and M. Stys. 2003. Identifying and Tracking Entity Mentions in a Maximum Entropy Framework. In ACL, editor, *Proceedings of the NAACL Workshop WordNet and Other Lexical Resources: Applications, Extensions and Customizations*.

G. Katz and F. Arosio. 2001. The annotation of temporal information in natural language sentences. In ACL, editor, *Proceedings of the 2001 ACL Workshop on Temporal and Spatial Information Processing*, pages 104–111, Toulouse, France.

A. Lavelli, B. Magnini, M. Negri, E. Pianta, M. Speranza, and R. Sprugnoli. 2005. Italian Content Annotation Bank (I-CAB): Temporal expressions (v. 1.0.): T-0505-12. Technical report, ITC-irst, Trento.

T. Moia. 2001. Telling apart temporal locating adverbials and time-denoting expressions. In ACL, editor, *Proceedings of the 2001 ACL Workshop on Temporal and Spatial Information Processing*, Toulouse, France.

M. Negri and L. Marseglia. 2004. Recognition and normalization of time expressions: Itc-irst at TERN 2004. Technical report, ITC-irst, Trento.

E. Saquete, P. Martínez-Barco, and R. Muñoz. 2004. Evaluation of the automatic multilinguality for time expression resolution. In *DEXA Workshops*, pages 25–30. IEEE Computer Society.

E. Saquete, R. Muñoz, and P. Martínez-Barco. 2005. Event ordering using terseo system. *Data and Knowledge Engineering Journal*, page (To be published).

E. Saquete. 2005. *Temporal information Resolution and its application to Temporal Question Answering*. Phd, Departamento de Lenguages y Sistemas Informáticos. Universidad de Alicante, June.

F. Schilder and C. Habel. 2001. From temporal expressions to temporal information: Semantic tagging of news messages. In ACL, editor, *Proceedings of the 2001 ACL Workshop on Temporal and Spatial Information Processing*, pages 65–72, Toulouse, France.

A. Setzer and R. Gaizauskas. 2002. On the importance of annotating event-event temporal relations in text. In LREC, editor, *Proceedings of the LREC Workshop on Temporal Annotation Standards, 2002*, pages 52–60, Las Palmas de Gran Canaria,Spain.

P. Vossen. 2000. EuroWordNet: Building a Multilingual Database with WordNets in 8 European Languages. *The ELRA Newsletter*, 5(1):9–10.

G. Wilson, I. Mani, B. Sundheim, and L. Ferro. 2001. A multilingual approach to annotating and extracting temporal information. In ACL, editor, *Proceedings of the 2001 ACL Workshop on Temporal and Spatial Information Processing*, pages 81–87, Toulouse, France.

A Framework for Incorporating Alignment Information in Parsing

Mark Hopkins
Dept. of Computational Linguistics
Saarland University
Saarbrücken, Germany
mhopkins@coli.uni-sb.de

Jonas Kuhn
Dept. of Computational Linguistics
Saarland University
Saarbrücken, Germany
jonask@coli.uni-sb.de

Abstract

The standard PCFG approach to parsing is quite successful on certain domains, but is relatively inflexible in the type of feature information we can include in its probabilistic model. In this work, we discuss preliminary work in developing a new probabilistic parsing model that allows us to easily incorporate many different types of features, including crosslingual information. We show how this model can be used to build a successful parser for a small handmade gold-standard corpus of 188 sentences (in 3 languages) from the Europarl corpus.

1 Introduction

Much of the current research into probabilistic parsing is founded on probabilistic context-free grammars (PCFGs) (Collins, 1999; Charniak, 2000; Charniak, 2001). For instance, consider the parse tree in Figure 1. One way to decompose this parse tree is to view it as a sequence of applications of CFG rules. For this particular tree, we could view it as the application of rule "NP → NP PP," followed by rule "NP → DT NN," followed by rule "DT → that," and so forth. Hence instead of analyzing $P(tree)$, we deal with the more modular:

P(NP → NP PP, NP → DT NN, DT → that, NN → money, PP → IN NP, IN → in, NP → DT NN, DT → the, NN → market)

Obviously this joint distribution is just as difficult to assess and compute with as $P(tree)$. However there exist cubic time algorithms to find the most likely parse if we assume that all CFG rule applications are marginally independent of one another. In other words, we need to assume that the above expression is equivalent to the following:

P(NP → NP PP) · P(NP → DT NN) · P(DT → that) · P(NN → money) · P(PP → IN NP) · P(IN → in) · P(NP → DT NN) · P(DT → the) · P(NN → market)

It is straightforward to assess the probability of the factors of this expression from a corpus using relative frequency. Then using these learned probabilities, we can find the most likely parse of a given sentence using the aforementioned cubic algorithms.

The problem, of course, with this simplification is that although it is computationally attractive, it is usually too strong of an independence assumption. To mitigate this loss of context, without sacrificing algorithmic tractability, typically researchers annotate the nodes of the parse tree with contextual information. For instance, it has been found to be useful to annotate nodes with their parent labels (Johnson, 1998), as shown in Figure 2. In this case, we would be learning probabilities like: P(PP-NP → IN-PP NP-PP).

The choice of which annotations to use is one of the main features that distinguish parsers based on this approach. Generally, this approach has proven quite effective in producing English phrase-structure grammar parsers that perform well on the Penn Treebank.

One drawback of this approach is that it is somewhat inflexible. Because we are adding probabilistic context by changing the data itself, we make our data increasingly sparse as we add features. Thus we are constrained from adding too

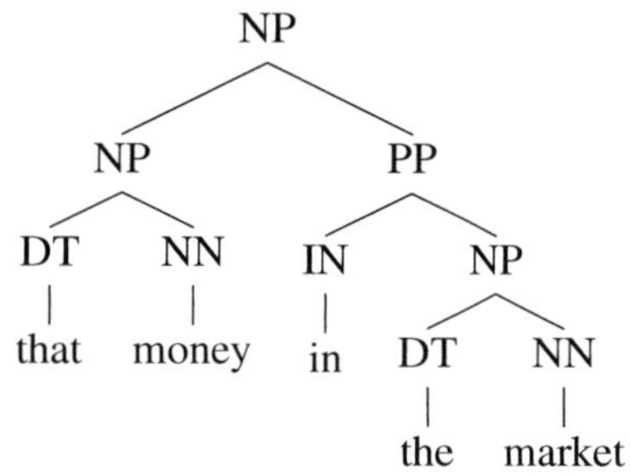

Figure 1: Example parse tree.

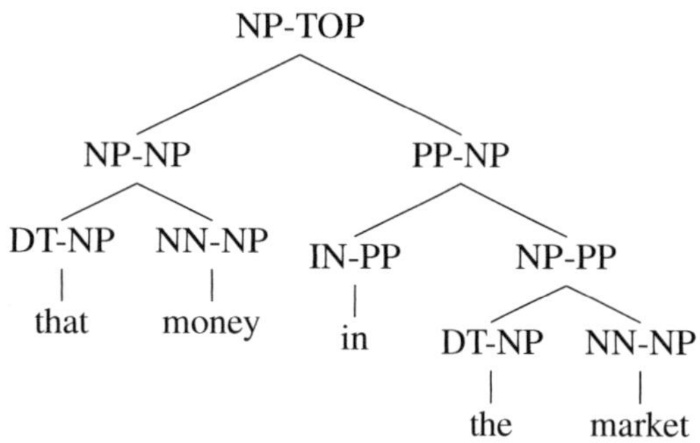

Figure 2: Example parse tree with parent annotations.

many features, because at some point we will not have enough data to sustain them. Hence in this approach, feature selection is not merely a matter of including good features. Rather, we must strike a delicate balance between how much context we want to include versus how much we dare to partition our data set.

This poses a problem when we have spent time and energy to find a good set of features that work well for a given parsing task on a given domain. For a different parsing task or domain, our parser may work poorly out-of-the-box, and it is no trivial matter to evaluate how we might adapt our feature set for this new task. Furthermore, if we gain access to a new source of feature information, then it is unclear how to incorporate such information into such a parser.

Namely, in this paper, we are interested in seeing how the cross-lingual information contained by sentence alignments can help the performance of a parser. We have a small gold-standard corpus of shallow-parsed parallel sentences (in English, French, and German) from the Europarl corpus. Because of the difficulty of testing new features using PCFG-based parsers, we propose a new probabilistic parsing framework that allows us to flexibly add features. The closest relative

	1	2	3	4	5
1	true	true	false	false	true
2	-	true	false	false	false
3	-	-	true	false	true
4	-	-	-	true	true
5	-	-	-	-	true

Figure 3: Span chart for example parse tree. Chart entry $(i, j) = true$ iff span (i, j) is a constituent in the tree.

of our framework is the maximum-entropy parser of Ratnaparkhi(Ratnaparkhi, 1997). Both frameworks are bottom-up, but while Ratnaparkhi's views parse trees as the sequence of applications of four different types of tree construction rules, our framework strives to be somewhat simpler and more general.

2 The Probability Model

The example parse tree in Figure 1 can also be decomposed in the following manner. First, we can represent the unlabeled tree with a boolean-valued chart (which we will call the *span chart*) that assigns the value of $true$ to a span if it is a constituent in the tree, and $false$ otherwise. The *span chart* for Figure 1 is shown in Figure 3.

To represent the labels, we simply add similar charts for each labeling scheme present in the tree. For a parse tree, there are typically three types of labels: words, preterminal tags, and nonterminals. Thus we need three labeling charts. Labeling charts for our example parse tree are depicted in Figure 4. Note that for words and preterminals, it is not really necessary to have a two-dimensional chart, but we do so here to motivate the general model.

The general model is as follows. Define a *labeling scheme* as a set of symbols including a special symbol $null$ (this will designate that a given span is unlabeled). For instance, we might define $L^{NT} = \{null, NP, PP, IN, DT\}$ to be a labeling scheme for non-terminals. Let $\mathcal{L} = \{L^1, L^2, ...L^m\}$ be a set of labeling schemes. Define a *model variable* of $\mathcal{L}$ as a symbol of the form S_{ij} or L^k_{ij}, for positive integers i, j, k, such that $j \geq i$ and $k \leq m$. The *domain* of model variable S_{ij} is $\{true, false\}$ (these variables indicate whether a given span is a tree constituent). The *domain* of model variable L^k_{ij} is L^k (these variables indicate which label from L^k is assigned to span

	1	2	3	4	5
1	that	null	null	null	null
2	-	money	null	null	null
3	-	-	in	null	null
4	-	-	-	the	null
5	-	-	-	-	market

	1	2	3	4	5
1	DT	null	null	null	null
2	-	NN	null	null	null
3	-	-	IN	null	null
4	-	-	-	DT	null
5	-	-	-	-	NN

	1	2	3	4	5
1	null	NP	null	null	NP
2	-	null	null	null	null
3	-	-	null	null	PP
4	-	-	-	null	NP
5	-	-	-	-	null

Figure 4: Labeling charts for example parse tree: the top chart is for word labels, the middle chart is for preterminal tag labels, and the bottom chart is for nonterminal labels. $null$ denotes an unlabeled span.

i, j). Define a *model order* of $\mathcal{L}$ as a total ordering Ω of the model variables of $\mathcal{L}$ such that for all i, j, k: $\Omega(S_{ij}) < \Omega(L_{ij}^k)$ (i.e. we decide whether a span is a constituent before attempting to label it). Let Ω_n denote the finite subset of Ω that includes precisely the model variables of the form S_{ij} or L_{ij}^k, where $j \leq n$.

Given a set $\mathcal{L}$ of labeling schemes and a model order Ω of $\mathcal{L}$, a preliminary generative story might look like the following:

1. Choose a positive integer n.

2. In the order defined by Ω_n, assign a value to every model variable of Ω_n from its domain, conditioned on any previous assignments made.

Thus some model order Ω for our example might instruct us to first choose whether span (4, 5) is a constituent, for which we might say "true," then instruct us to choose a label for that constituent, for which we might say "NP," and so forth.

There are a couple of problems with this generative story. One problem is that it allows us to make structural decisions that do not result in a well-formed tree. For instance, we should not be permitted to assign the value $true$ to both variable S_{13} and S_{24}. Generally, we cannot allow two model variables S_{ij} and S_{kl} to both be assigned $true$ if they *properly overlap*, i.e. their spans overlap and one is not a subspan of the other. We should also ensure that the leaves and the root are considered constituents. Another problem is that it allows us to make labeling decisions that do not correspond with our chosen structure. It should not be possible to label a span which is not a constituent.

With this in mind, we revise our generative story.

1. Choose a positive integer n from distribution P_0.

2. In the order defined by Ω_n, process model variable x of Ω_n:

   (a) If $x = S_{ij}$, then:

      i. Automatically assign the value $false$ if there exists a properly overlapping model variable S_{kl} such that S_{kl} has already been assigned the value $true$.

      ii. Automatically assign the value $true$ if $i = j$ or if $i = 1$ and $j = n$.

      iii. Otherwise assign a value s_{ij} to S_{ij} from its domain, drawn from some probability distribution P_S conditioned on all previous variable assignments.

   (b) If $x = L_{ij}^k$, then:

      i. Automatically assign the value $null$ to L_{ij}^k if S_{ij} was assigned the value $false$ (note that this is well-defined because of way we defined model order).

      ii. Otherwise assign a value l_{ij}^k to L_{ij}^k from its domain, drawn from some probability distribution P_k conditioned on all previous variable assignments.

Defining $\Omega_n^<(x) = \{y \in \Omega_n | \Omega(y) < \Omega(x)\}$ for $x \in \Omega_n$, we can decompose $P(tree)$ into the following expression:

$$P_0(n) \cdot \prod_{S_{ij} \in \Omega_n} P_S(s_{ij} | n, \Omega_n^<(S_{ij})) \cdot \prod_{L_{ij}^k \in \Omega_n} P_k(l_{ij}^k | n, \Omega_n^<(L_{ij}^k))$$

where P_S and P_k obey the constraints given in the generative story above (e.g. $P_S(S_{ii} = true) = 1$, etc.)

Obviously it is impractical to learn conditional distributions over every conceivable history, so instead we choose a small set $\mathbf{F}$ of feature variables, and provide a set of functions $\mathcal{F}_n$ that map every partial history of Ω_n to some feature vector $\mathbf{f} \in \mathbf{F}$ (later we will see examples of such feature functions). Then we make the assumption that:

$$P_S(s_{ij} | n, \Omega_n^<(S_{ij}) = P_S(s_{ij} | \mathbf{f})$$

where $\mathbf{f} = \mathcal{F}_n(\Omega_n^<(S_{ij}))$ and that

$$P_k(l_{ij}^k | n, \Omega_n^<(S_{ij}) = P_k(l_{ij}^k | \mathbf{f})$$

where $\mathbf{f} = \mathcal{F}_n(\Omega_n^<(L_{ij}^k))$.

In this way, our learning task is simplified to learn functions $P_0(n)$, $P_S(s_{ij}|\mathbf{f})$, and $P_k(l_{ij}^k|\mathbf{f})$. Given a corpus of labeled trees, it is straightforward to extract the training instances for these distributions and then use these instances to learn distributions using one's preferred learning method (e.g., maximum entropy models or decision trees).

For this paper, we are interested in parse trees which have three labeling schemes. Let $\mathcal{L} = \{L^{word}, L^{PT}, L^{NT}\}$, where L^{word} is a labeling scheme for words, L^{PT} is a labeling scheme for preterminals, and L^{NT} is a labeling scheme for nonterminals. We will define model order Ω such that:

1. $\Omega(S_{ij}) < \Omega(L_{ij}^{word}) < \Omega(L_{ij}^{PT}) < \Omega(L_{ij}^{NT})$.
2. $\Omega(L_{ij}^{NT}) < \Omega(S_{kl})$ iff $j - i < l - k$ or $(j - i = l - k$ and $i < k)$.

In this work, we are not as much interested in learning a marginal distribution over parse trees, but rather a conditional distribution for parse trees, given a tagged sentence (from which n is also known). We will assume that P_{word} is conditionally independent of all the other model variables, given n and the L_{ij}^{word} variables. We will also assume that P_{pt} is conditionally independent of the other model variables, given n, the L_{ij}^{word} variables, and the L_{ij}^{pt} variables. These assumptions allow us to express $P(tree | n, L_{ij}^{word}, L_{ij}^{pt})$ as the following:

$$\prod_{S_{ij} \in \Omega_n} P_S(s_{ij} | \mathbf{f}_S) \cdot \prod_{L_{ij}^{nt} \in \Omega_n} P_{nt}(l_{ij}^{nt} | \mathbf{f}_{nt})$$

where $\mathbf{f}_S = \mathcal{F}_n(\Omega_n^<(S_{ij}))$ and $\mathbf{f}_{nt} = \mathcal{F}_n(\Omega_n^<(L_{ij}^{nt}))$. Hence our learning task in this paper will be to learn the probability distributions $P_S(s_{ij}|\mathbf{f}_S)$ and $P_{nt}(l_{ij}^{nt}|\mathbf{f}_{nt})$, for some choice of feature functions $\mathcal{F}_n$.

3 Decoding

For the PCFG parsing model, we can find $argmax_{tree} P(tree|sentence)$ using a cubic-time dynamic programming-based algorithm. By adopting a more flexible probabilistic model, we sacrifice polynomial-time guarantees. Nevertheless, we can still devise search algorithms that work efficiently in practice. For the decoding of the probabilistic model of the previous section, we choose a depth-first branch-and-bound approach, specifically because of two advantages. First, this approach is linear space. Second, it is anytime, i.e. it finds a (typically good) solution early and improves this solution as the search progresses. Thus if one does not wish the spend the time to run the search to completion (and ensure optimality), one can use this algorithm easily as a heuristic.

The search space is simple to define. Given a set $\mathcal{L}$ of labeling schemes and a model order Ω of $\mathcal{L}$, the search algorithm simply makes assignments to the model variables (depth-first) in the order defined by Ω.

This search space can clearly grow to be quite large, however in practice the search speed is improved drastically by using branch-and-bound backtracking. Namely, at any choice point in the search space, we first choose the least cost child to expand. In this way, we quickly obtain a greedy solution. After that point, we can continue to keep track of the best solution we have found so far, and if at any point we reach an internal node of our search tree with partial cost greater than the total cost of our best solution, we can discard this node and discontinue exploration of that subtree. This technique can result in a significant aggregate savings of computation time, depending on

EN: [$_1$ [$_2$ On behalf of the European People 's Party ,] [$_3$ I] call [$_5$ for a vote [$_6$ in favour of that motion]]]

FR: [$_1$ [$_2$ Au nom du Parti populaire européen ,] [$_3$ je] demande [$_5$ l' adoption [$_6$ de cette résolution]]]

DE: [$_1$ [$_2$ Im Namen der Europäischen Volkspartei] rufe [$_3$ ich] [$_4$ Sie] auf , [$_5$ [$_6$ diesem Entschließungsantrag] zuzustimmen]]

ES: [$_1$ [$_2$ En nombre del Grupo del Partido Popular Europeo ,] solicito [$_5$ la aprobación [$_6$ de la resolución]]]

Figure 5: Annotated sentence tuple

the nature of the cost function. For our limited parsing domain, it appears to perform quite well, taking fractions of a second to parse each sentence (which are short, with a maximum of 20 words per sentence).

4 Experiments

Our parsing domain is based on a "lean" phrase correspondence representation for multitexts from parallel corpora (i.e., tuples of sentences that are translations of each other). We defined an annotation scheme that focuses on translational correspondence of *phrasal units* that have a distinct, language-independent *semantic status*. It is a hypothesis of our longer-term project that such a semantically motivated, relatively coarse phrase correspondence relation is most suitable for weakly supervised approaches to parsing of large amounts of parallel corpus data. Based on this lean phrase structure format, we intend to explore an alternative to the annotation projection approach to cross-linguistic bootstrapping of parsers by (Hwa et al., 2005). They depart from a standard treebank parser for English, "projecting" its analyses to another language using word alignments over a parallel corpus. Our planned bootstrapping approach will not start out with a given parser for English (or any other language), but use a small set of manually annotated seed data following the lean phrase correspondence scheme, and then bootstrap consensus representations on large amounts of unannotated multitext data. At the present stage, we only present experiments for training an initial system on a set of seed data.

The annotation scheme underlying in the gold standard annotation consists of (A) a bracketing for each language and (B) a correspondence relation of the constituents across languages. Neither the constituents nor the embedding or correspondent relations were labelled.

The guiding principle for bracketing (A) is very simple: all and only the units that clearly play the role of a semantic argument or modifier in a larger unit are bracketed. This means that function words, light verbs, "bleeched" PPs like *in spite of* etc. are included with the content-bearing elements. This leads to a relatively flat bracketing structure. Referring or quantified expressions that may include adjectives and possessive NPs or PPs are also bracketed as single constituents (e.g., [*the president of France*]), unless the semantic relations reflected by the internal embedding are part of the predication of the sentence. A few more specific annotation rules were specified for cases like coordination and discontinuous constituents.

The correspondence relation (B) is guided by semantic correspondence of the bracketed units; the mapping need not preserve the tree structure. Neither does a constituent need to have a correspondent in all (or any) of the other languages (since the content of this constituent may be implicit in other languages, or subsumed by the content of another constituent). "Semantic correspondence" is not restricted to truth-conditional equivalence, but is generalized to situations where two units just serve the same rhetorical function in the original text and the translation.

Figure 5 is an annotation example. Note that index 4 (the audience addressed by the speaker) is realized overtly only in German (*Sie* 'you'); in Spanish, index 3 is realized only in the verbal inflection (which is not annotated). A more detailed discussion of the annotation scheme is presented in (Kuhn and Jellinghaus, to appear).

For the current parsing experiments, only the bracketing within each of three languages (English, French, German) is used; the cross-linguistic phrase correspondences are ignored (although we intend to include them in future experiments). We automatically tagged the training and test data in English, French, and German with Schmid's decision-tree part-of-speech tagger (Schmid, 1994).

The training data were taken from the sentence-aligned Europarl corpus and consisted of 188 sentences for each of the three languages, with max-

Feature Notation	Description
p(*language*)	the preterminal tag of word $x-1$ (*null* if does not exist)
f(*language*)	the preterminal tag of word x
l(*language*)	the preterminal tag of word y
n(*language*)	the preterminal tag of word $y-1$ (*null* if does not exist)
lng	the length of the span (i.e. $y-x+1$)

Figure 6: Features for span (x, y). E = English, F = French, G = German

English features	Crosslingual features	Rec.	Prec.	F-score	No cross
p(E), f(E), l(E)	none	40.3	63.6	49.4 ($\pm 3.9\%$)	57.1
	p(F), f(F), l(F)	43.1	67.6	52.6 ($\pm 4.0\%$)	61.2
	p(G), f(G), l(G)	45.9	66.8	54.4 ($\pm 4.0\%$)	69.4
	p(F), f(F), l(F), p(G), f(G), l(G)	44.5	65.5	53.0 ($\pm 3.9\%$)	65.3
p(E), f(E), l(E), n(E)	none	57.2	68.6	62.4 ($\pm 4.0\%$)	65.3
	p(F), f(F), l(F), n(F)	56.6	71.9	63.3 ($\pm 4.0\%$)	75.5
	p(G), f(G), l(G), n(G)	57.9	67.7	62.5 ($\pm 3.9\%$)	67.3
	p(F), f(F), l(F), n(F), p(G), f(G), l(G), n(G)	57.9	72.1	64.2 ($\pm 4.0\%$)	77.6
p(E), f(E), l(E), n(E), lng	none	64.8	71.2	67.9 ($\pm 4.0\%$)	79.6
	p(F), f(F), l(F), n(F), lng	62.1	74.4	67.7 ($\pm 4.0\%$)	83.7
	p(G), f(G), l(G), n(G), lng	61.4	78.8	69.0 ($\pm 4.1\%$)	83.7
	p(F), f(F), l(F), n(F), p(G), f(G), l(G), n(G), lng	63.1	76.9	69.3 ($\pm 4.1\%$)	81.6
	BIKEL	57.9	60.2	59.1 ($\pm 3.8\%$)	57.1

Figure 7: Parsing results for various feature sets, and the Bikel baseline. The F-scores are annotated with 95% confidence intervals.

imal length of 21 words in English (French: 38; German: 24) and an average length of 14.0 words in English (French 16.8; German 13.6). The test data were 50 sentences for each language, picked arbitrarily with the same length restrictions. The training and test data were manually aligned following the guidelines.[1]

For the word alignments used as learning features, we used GIZA++, relying on the default parameters. We trained the alignments on the full Europarl corpus for both directions of each language pair.

As a baseline system we trained Bikel's reimplementation (Bikel, 2004) of Collins' parser (Collins, 1999) on the gold standard (English) training data, applying a simple additional smoothing procedure for the modifier events in order to counteract some obvious data sparseness issues.[2]

Since we were attempting to learn unlabeled trees, in this experiment we only needed to learn the probabilistic model of Section 3 with no labeling schemes. Hence we need only to learn the probability distribution:

$$P_S(s_{ij}|\mathbf{f}_S)$$

In other words, we need to learn the probability that a given span is a tree constituent, given some set of features of the words and preterminal tags of the sentences, as well as the previous span decisions we have made. The main decision that

[1] A subset of 39 sentences was annotated by two people independently, leading to an F-Score in bracketing agreement between 84 and 90 for the three languages. Since finding an annotation scheme that works well in the bootstrapping set-up is an issue on our research agenda, we postpone a more detailed analysis of the annotation process until it becomes clear that a particular scheme is indeed useful.

[2] For the nonterminal labels, we defined the left-most lexical daughter in each local subtree of depth 1 to project its part-of-speech category to the phrase level and introduced a special nonterminal label for the rare case of nonterminal nodes dominating no preterminal node.

remains, then, is which feature set to use. The features we employ are very simple. Namely, for span (i, j) we consider the preterminal tags of words $i - 1$, i, j, and $j + 1$, as well as the French and German preterminal tags of the words to which these English words align. Finally, we also use the length of the span as a feature. The features considered are summarized in Figure 6.

To learn the conditional probability distribututions, we choose to use maximum entropy models because of their popularity and the availability of software packages. Specifically, we use the MEGAM package (Daumé III, 2004) from USC/ISI.

We did experiments for a number of different feature sets, with and without alignment features. The results (precision, recall, F-score, and the percentage of sentences with no cross-bracketing) are summarized in Figure 7. Note that with a very simple set of features (the previous, first, last, and next preterminal tags of the sequence), our parser performs on par with the Bikel baseline. Adding the length of the sequence as a feature increases the quality of the parser to a statistically significant difference over the baseline. The crosslingual information provided (which is admittedly naive) does not provide a statistically significant improvement over the vanilla set of features. The conclusion to be drawn is not that crosslingual information does not help (such a conclusion should not be drawn from the meager set of crosslingual features we have used here for demonstration purposes). Rather, the take-away point is that such information can be easily incorporated using this framework.

5 Discussion

One of the primary concerns about this framework is speed, since the decoding algorithm for our probabilistic model is not polynomial-time like the decoding algorithms for PCFG parsing. Nevertheless, in our experiments with shallow parsed 20-word sentences, time was not a factor. Furthermore, in our ongoing research applying this probabilistic framework to the task of Penn Treebank-style parsing, this approach appears to also be viable for the 40-word sentences of Sections 22 and 23 of the WSJ treebank. A strong mitigating factor of the theoretical intractibility is the fact that we have an *anytime* decoding algorithm, hence even in cases when we cannot run the algorithm to completion (for a guaranteed optimal solution), the algorithm always returns some solution, the quality of which increases over time. Hence we can tell the algorithm how much time it has to compute, and it will return the best solution it can compute in that time frame.

This work suggests that one can get a good quality parser for a new parsing domain with relatively little effort (the features we chose are extremely simple and certainly could be improved on). The cross-lingual information that we used (namely, the foreign preterminal tags of the words to which our span was aligned by GIZA) did not give a significant improvement to our parser. However the goal of this work was not to make definitive statements about the value of crosslingual features in parsing, but rather to show a framework in which such crosslingual information could be easily incorporated and exploited. We believe we have provided the beginnings of one in this work, and work continues on finding more complex features that will improve performance well beyond the baseline.

Acknowledgement

The work reported in this paper was supported by the *Deutsche Forschungsgemeinschaft* (DFG; German Research Foundation) in the Emmy Noether project PTOLEMAIOS on grammar learning from parallel corpora.

References

Daniel M. Bikel. 2004. Intricacies of collins' parsing model. *Computational Linguistics*, 30(4):479–511.

Eugene Charniak. 2000. A maximum entropy-inspired parser. In *NAACL*.

Eugene Charniak. 2001. Immediate-head parsing for language models. In *ACL*.

Michael Collins. 1999. *Head-driven statistical models for natural language parsing*. Ph.D. thesis, University of Pennsylvania.

Hal Daumé III. 2004. Notes on CG and LM-BFGS optimization of logistic regression. Paper available at http://www.isi.edu/ hdaume/docs/daume04cg-bfgs.ps, implementation available at http://www.isi.edu/ hdaume/megam/, August.

Rebecca Hwa, Philip Resnik, Amy Weinberg, Clara Cabezas, and Okan Kolak. 2005. Bootstrapping parsers via syntactic projection across parallel texts. *Natural Language Engineering*, 11(3):311–325.

Mark Johnson. 1998. PCFG models of linguistic tree representation. *Computational Linguistics*, 24:613–632.

Jonas Kuhn and Michael Jellinghaus. to appear. Multilingual parallel treebanking: a lean and flexible approach. In *Proceedings of the Fifth International Conference on Language Resources and Evaluation*, Genoa, Italy.

Adwait Ratnaparkhi. 1997. A linear observed time statistical parser based on maximum entropy models. In *EMNLP*.

Helmut Schmid. 1994. Probabilistic part-of-speech tagging using decision trees. In *International Conference on New Methods in Language Processing*.

Induction of Cross-Language Affix and Letter Sequence Correspondence

Ari Rappoport
Institute of Computer Science
The Hebrew University
www.cs.huji.ac.il/~arir

Tsahi Levent-Levi
Institute of Computer Science
The Hebrew University

Abstract

We introduce the problem of explicit modeling of form relationships between words in different languages, focusing here on languages having an alphabetic writing system and affixal morphology. We present an algorithm that learns the cross-language correspondence between affixes and letter sequences. The algorithm does not assume prior knowledge of affixes in any of the languages, using only a simple single letter correspondence as seed. Results are given for the English-Spanish language pair.

1 Introduction

Studying various relationships between languages is a central task in computational linguistics, with many application areas. In this paper we introduce the problem of induction of form relationships between words in different languages. More specifically, we focus on languages having an alphabetic writing system and affixal morphology, and we construct a model for the cross-language correspondence between letter sequences and between affixes. Since the writing system is alphabetic, letter sequences are highly informative regarding sound sequences as well.

Concretely, the model is designed to answer the following question: what are the affixes and letter sequences in one language that correspond frequently to similar entities in another language? Such a model has obvious applications to the construction of learning materials in language education and to statistical machine translation.

The input to our algorithm consists of word pairs from two languages, a sizeable fraction of which is assumed to be related graphemically and affixally. The algorithm has three main stages. First, an alignment between the word pairs is computed by an EM algorithm that uses an edit distance metric based on an increasingly refined individual letter correspondence cost function. Second, affix pair candidates are discovered and ranked, based on a language independent abstract model of affixal morphology. Third, letter sequences that correspond productively in the two languages are discovered and ranked by EM iterations that use a cost function based on the discovered affixes and on compatibility of alignments.

The affix learning part of the algorithm is totally unsupervised, in that we do not assume knowledge of affixes in any of the single languages involved. The letter sequence learning part utilizes a simple initial correspondence between individual letters, and the rest of its operation is unsupervised.

We believe that this is the first paper that explicitly addresses cross-language morphology, and the first that presents a comprehensive inter-language word form correspondence model that combines morphology and letter sequences.

Section 2 motivates the problem and defines it in detail. In Section 3 we discuss relevant previous work. The algorithm is presented in Section 4, and results for English-Spanish in Section 5.

2 Problem Motivation and Definition

We would like to discover characteristics of word form correspondence between languages. In this section we discuss what exactly this means and why it is useful.

Word form. Word forms have at least three different aspects: sound, writing system, and internal structure, corresponding to the linguistics fields of phonology, orthography and morphology. When the writing system is phonetically based, the written form of a word is highly informative of how the word sounds. Individual writing units are referred to as graphemes.

Morphology studies the internal structure of words when viewed as comprised of semantics carrying components. Morphological units can be classified into two general classes, stems (or roots) and bound morphemes, which combine to create words using various kinds of operators. The linear affixing operator combines stems and bound morphemes (affixes) using linear ordering with possible fusion effects, usually at the seams.

Word form correspondence. In this paper we study cross-language word form correspondence. We should first ask why there should be any relationship at all between word forms in different languages. There are at least two factors that create such relationships. First, languages may share a common ancestor. Second, languages may borrow words, writing systems and even morphological operators from each other. Note that usage of proper names can be viewed as a kind of borrowing. In both cases form relationships are accompanied by semantic relatedness. Words that possess a degree of similarity of form and meaning are usually termed *cognates*.

Our goal in examining word forms in different languages is to identify correspondence phenomena that could be useful for certain applications. These would usually be correspondence similarities that are common to many word pairs.

Problem statement for the present paper. For reasons of paper length, we focus here on languages having the following two characteristics. First, we assume an alphabetic writing system. This implies that grapheme correspondences will be highly informative of sound correspondences as well. From now on we will use the term 'letter' instead of 'grapheme'. Second, we assume linear affixal morphology (prefixing and suffixing), which is an extremely frequent morphological operator in many languages.

We address the two fundamental word form entities in languages that obey those assumptions: affixes and letter sequences. Our goal is to discover frequent cross-language pairs of those entities and quantify the correspondence. Pairing of letter sequences is expected to be mostly due to regular sound transformations and spelling conventions. Pairing of affixes could be due to morphological principles – predictable relationships between the affixing operators (their form and meaning) – or, again, due to sound transformations and spelling.

The input to the algorithm consists of a set of ordered pairs of words, one from each language. We do not assume that all input word pairs exhibit the correspondence relationships of interest, but obviously the quality of results will depend on the fraction of the pair set that does exhibit them. A particular word may participate in more than a single pair. As explained above, the relationships of interest to us in this paper usually imply semantic affinity between the words; hence, a suitable pair set can be generated by selecting word pairs that are possible translations of each other. Practical ways to obtain such pairs are using a bilingual dictionary or a word aligned parallel corpus. We had used the former, which implies that we addressed only derivational, not inflectional, morphology. Using a dictionary provides a kind of semantic supervision that allows us to focus on the desired form relationships.

We also assume that the algorithm is provided with a prototypical individual letter mapping as seed. Such a mapping is trivial to obtain in virtually all practical situations, either because both languages utilize the same alphabet or by using a manually prepared, coarse alphabet mapping (e.g., anybody even shallowly familiar with Cyrillic or Semitic scripts can prepare such a mapping in just a few minutes.)

We do not assume knowledge of affixes in any of the languages. Our algorithm is thus fully unsupervised in terms of morphology and very weakly seeded in term of orthography.

Motivating applications. There are two main applications that motivate our research. In second language education, a major challenge for adult learners is the high memory load due to the huge number of lexical items in a language. Item memorization is known to be greatly assisted by tying items with existing knowledge (Matlin02). When learning a second language lexicon, it is beneficial to consciously note similarities between new and known words. Discovering and explaining such similarities automatically would help teachers in preparing reliable study materials, and learners in remembering words.

Recognition of familiar components also helps learners when encountering previously unseen words. For example, suppose an English speaker who learns Spanish and sees the word 'parcialmente'. A word form correspondence model would tell her that 'mente' is an affix strongly corresponding to the English 'ly', and that the letter pair 'ci' often corresponds to the English 'ti'. The model thus enables guessing or recalling the English word 'partially'.

Our model could also warn the learner of cognates that are possibly false, by recognizing similar words that are not paired in the dictionary.

A second application area is machine translation. Both cognate identification (Kondrak et al 03) and morphological information in one of the languages (Niessen00) have been proven useful in statistical machine translation.

3 Previous Work

Cross-language models for phonology and orthography have been developed for back-transliteration in cross-lingual information retrieval (CLIR), mostly from Japanese and Chinese to English. (Knight98) uses a series of weighted finite state transducers, each focusing on a particular mapping. (Lin02) uses minimal edit distance with a 'confusion matrix' that models phonetic similarity. (Li04, Bilac04) generalize using the sequence alignment algorithm presented in (Brill00) for spelling correction. (Bilac04) explicitly separates the phonemic and graphemic models. None of that work addresses morphology and in all of it grapheme and phoneme correspondence is only a transient tool which is not studied on its own. (Mueller05) explicitly models phonological similarities between related languages, but does not address morphology and orthography.

Cognate identification has been studied in computational historical linguistics. (Covington96, Kondrak03a) use a fixed, manually determined single entity mapping. (Kondrak03b) generalizes to letter sequences based on the algorithm in (Melamed97). The results are good for the historical linguistics application. However, morphology is not addressed, and the sequence correspondence model is less powerful than that employed in the back-transliteration and spelling correction literature. In addition, all effects that occur at word endings, including suffixes, are completely ignored. (Mackay05) presents good results for cognate identification using a word similarity measure based on pair hidden Markov models. Again, morphology was not modeled explicitly.

A nice application for cross-language morphology is (Schulz04), which acquires a Spanish medical lexicon from a Portuguese seed lexicon using a manually prepared table of 842 Spanish affixes.

Unsupervised learning of affixal morphology in a single language is a heavily researched problem. (Medina00) studies several methods, including the squares method we use in Section 4. (Goldsmith01) presents an impressive system that searches for 'signatures', which can be viewed as generalized squares. (Creutz04) presents a very general method that excels at dealing with highly inflected languages. (Wicentowsky04) deals with inflectional and irregular morphology by using semantic similarity between stem and stem+affix, also addressing stem-affix fusion effects. None of these papers deals with cross-language morphology.

4 The Algorithm

Overview. Letter sequences and affixes are different entities exhibiting different correspondence phenomena, hence are addressed at separate stages. The result of addressing one will assist us in addressing the other.

The fundamental tool that we use to discover correspondence effects is alignment of the two words in a pair. Stage 1 of the algorithm creates an alignment using the given coarse individual letter mapping, which is simultaneously improved to a much more accurate one.

Stage 2 discovers affix pairs using a general language independent affixal morphology model.

In stage 3 we utilize the improved individual letter relation from stage 1 and the affix pairs discovered in stage 2 to create a general letter sequence mapping, again using word alignments. In the following we describe in detail each of these stages.

Initial alignment. The main goal of stage 1 is to align the letters of each word pair. This is done by a standard minimal edit distance algorithm, efficiently implemented using dynamic programming (Gusfield97, Ristad98). We use the standard edit distance operations of replace, insert and delete. The letter mapping given as input defines a cost matrix where replacement of corresponding letters has a low (0) cost and of all others a high (1) cost. The cost of insert and delete is arbitrarily set to be the same as that of replacing non-identical letters. We use a hash table rather than a matrix, to prepare for later stages of the algorithm.

When the correspondence between the languages is very high, this initial alignment can already provide acceptable results for the next stage. However, in order to increase the accuracy of the alignment we now refine the letter cost matrix by employing an EM algorithm that iteratively updates the cost matrix using the current alignment and computes an improved alignment based on the updated cost matrix (Brill00, Lin02, Li04, Bilac04). The cost of mapping a letter K to a letter L is updated to be proportional to the count of this mapping in all of the current alignments divided by the total number of mappings of the letter K.

Affix pairs. The computed letter alignment assists us in addressing affixes. Recall that we possess no knowledge of affixes; hence, we need to discover not only pairing of affixes, but the participating affixes as well. Our algorithm discovers affixes and their pairing simultaneously. It is inspired by the squares algorithm for affix learning in a single language (Medina00)[1].

The squares method assumes that affixes generally combine with very many stems, and that stems are generally utilized more than once. These assumptions are due to a functional view of affixal morphology as a process whose goal is to create a large number of word forms using fewer parameters. A stem that combines with an affix is quite likely to also appear alone, so the empty affix is allowed.

We first review the method as it is used in a single language. Given a word W=AB (where A and B are non-empty letter sequences), our task is to measure how likely it is for B to be a suffix (prefix learning is similar.) We refer to AB as a *segmentation* of W, using a hyphen to show segmentations of concrete words. Define a *square* to be four words (including W) of the forms W=AB, U=AD, V=CB, and Y=CD (one of the letter sequences C, D is allowed to be empty.)

Such a square might attest that B, D are suffixes and that A, C are stems. However, we must be careful: it might also attest that B, D are stems and A, C are prefixes. A square attests for a segmentation, not for a particular labeling of its components.

As an example, if W is 'talking', a possible square is {talk-ing, hold-ing, talk-s, hold-s} where A=talk, B=ing, C=hold, and D=s. Another possible square is {talk-ing, danc-ing, talk-ed, danc-ed}, where A=talk, B=ing, C=danc, and D=ed. This demonstrates a drawback of the method, namely its sensitivity to spelling; C with the empty suffix is written 'dance', not 'danc'. The four words {talking, dancing, talk, dance} do not form a square.

We now count the number of squares in which B appears. If this number is relatively large (which needs to be precisely defined), we have a strong evidence that B is a suffix or a stem. We can distinguish between these two cases using the number of *witnesses* – actual words in which B appears.

We generalize the squares method to the discovery of cross-language affix pairs, as follows. We now use W to denote not a single word but a word pair W1:W2. B does not denote a suffix candidate but a suffix pair candidate, B1:B2, and similarly for D. A and C denote stem pair candidates A1:A2 and C1:C2, respectively.

We now define a key concept. Given a word pair W=W1:W2 aligned under an alignment T, two segmentations W1=A1B1 and W2=A2B2 are said to be *compatible* if no alignment line of T connects a subset of A1 to a subset of B2 or a subset of A2 to a subset of B1. This definition is also applicable to alignments between letter sequences.

We now impose our key requirement: for all of the words involved in the cross-lingual square, their segmentations into two parts must be compatible under the alignment computed at stage 1.

For example, consider the English-Spanish word pair affirmation : afirmacion. The segmentation affirma-tion : afirma-cion is attested by the square

A1B1 : A2B2 = affirma-tion : afirma-cion

A1D1 : A2D2 = affirma-tively : afirma-tivamente

C1B1 : C2B2 = coopera-tion : coopera-cion

C1D1 : C2D2 = coopera-tively : coopera-tivamente

assuming that the appropriate parts are aligned. Note that 'tively' is comprised of two smaller affixes, but the squares method legitimately considers it an affix by itself. Note also that since all of A1, A2, C1 and C2 end with the same letter, that letter can be moved to the beginning of B1, B2, D1, D2 to produce a different square (affirm-ation : afirm-acion, etc.) from the same four word pairs.

Since we have no initial reason to favor a particular affix candidate over another, and since the total computational cost is not prohibitive, we

[1] (Medina00) attributes the algorithm to Joseph Greenberg.

now simply count the number of attesting squares for *all* possible compatible segmentations of all word pairs, and sort the list according to the number of witnesses. To reduce noise, we remove affix candidates for which the absolute number of witnesses or squares is small (e.g., ten.)

Letter sequences. The third and last stage of the algorithm discovers letter sequences that correspond frequently. This is again done by an edit distance algorithm, generalizing that of stage 1 so that sequences longer than a single letter can be replaced, inserted or deleted. In order to reduce noise, prior to that we remove word pairs whose stems are very different. Those are identified by comparing their edit distance costs, which should hence be normalized according to length (of the longer stem in a pair.) Note that accuracy is increased by considering only stems: affix pairs might be very different, thus might increase edit distance cost even when the stems do exhibit good sequence pairing effects.

When generalizing the edit distance algorithm, we need to specify which letter sequences will be considered, because it does not make sense to consider all possible mappings of all subsets to all possible subsets – the number of different such pairs will be too large to show any meaningful statistics.

The letter sequences considered were obtained by 'fattening' the lines in alignments yielding minimal edit distances, using an EM algorithm as done in (Brill00, Bilac04, Li04). The details of the algorithm can be found in these papers. The most important step, line fattening, is done as follows. We examine all alignment lines, each connecting two letter sequences (initially, of length 1.) We unite those sequences with adjacent sequences in all ways that are compatible with the alignment, and add the new sequences to the cost function to be used in the next EM iteration.

If we kept letter sequence pairs that are not frequent in the cost function, they would distort the counts of more frequent letter sequences with which they partially overlap. We thus need to retain only some of the sequence pairs discovered. We have experimented with several ways to do that, all yielding quite similar results. For the results presented in this paper, we used the idea that sequences that clearly map to specific sequences are more important to our model than sequences that 'fuzzily' map to many sequences. To quantify this approach, for each language-1 sequence we sorted the corresponding language-2 sequences according to count, and removed pairs in which the language-2 item was responsible for only a small percentage of the total (we used a threshold of 0.05). We further removed sequence pairs whose absolute counts are low.

Discussion. We deal with affixes before sequences because, as we have seen, identification of affixes helps us in identifying sequences, while the opposite order actually hurts us: sequences sometimes contain letters from both stem and affix, which invalidates squares that are otherwise valid.

It may be asked why the squares stage is needed at all – perhaps affixes would be discovered anyway as sequences in stage 3. Our assumption was that affixes are best discovered using properties resulting from their very nature. We have experimented with the option of removing stage 2 and discovering affixes as letter sequences in stage 3, and verified that it gives markedly lower quality results. Even the very frequent pair -ly:-mente was not signaled out, because its count was lowered by those of the pairs -ly:-ente, -ly:nte, -y:-te, etc.

5 Results

We have run the algorithm on several language pairs using affixal morphology and the Latin alphabet: English vs. Spanish, Portuguese and Italian, and Spanish vs. Portuguese. All of them are related both historically and through borrowing (obviously at varying degrees), so we expect relatively many correspondence phenomena. Testing results for one of these pairs, English – Spanish, are presented in this section.

The input word pair set was created from a bilingual dictionary (Freelang04) by taking all translations of single English words to single Spanish words, generating about 13,000 word pairs.

Individual letter mapping. The cost matrix after EM convergence (25 iterations) exhibits the following phenomena (e:s (c) denotes that the final cost of replacing the English letter e by the Spanish letter s is c): (1) English letters mostly map to identical Spanish letters, apart from letters that Spanish does not make use of like k and w; (2) some English vowels map frequently to some Spanish vowels: y maps almost exclusively to i (0.01), e:a (0.47) is highly productive, e:o (0.98), i:e (0.97), e:o (0.98); (3) some English consonants map to different Spanish ones: t:c

(0.89) (due to an affix, -tion:-cion); m:n (0.44) is highly frequent; b:v(0.80); x:j (0.78), x:s(0.94); w always maps to v; j:y (0.11); (4) h usually disappears, h:NULL (0.13); and (5) inserted Spanish letters include the vowels o, e, a and i, at that order, where o overwhelms the others. The English o maps exclusively to the Spanish o and not to other vowels.

Affixes. Table 1 shows some of the conspicuous affix pairs discovered by the algorithm. We show both the number of witnesses and of squares.

The table shows many interesting correspondence phenomena. However, discussing those at depth from a linguistic point of view is out of the scope of this paper. Some notes: (1) some of the most frequent affix pairs are not that close orthographically: -ity:-idad, -ness:- (nouns), -ate:-ar (verbs), -ly-:-mente (adverbs), -al:-o (adjectives), so will not necessarily be found using ordinary edit distance methods; (2) some affixes are ranked high both with and without a letter that they favor when attaching to a stem: -ation:-acion, -ate:-ar; (3) some English suffixes map strongly to several Spanish ones: -er:-o, -er:-ador.

Recall that the table cannot include inflectional affixes, since our input was taken from a bilingual dictionary, not from a text corpus.

Letter sequences. Table 2 shows some nice pairings, stemming from all three expected phenomena: st-:est- (due to phonology), ph:f, th:t, ll:l (due to orthography), and tion:cion, tia:cia (due to morphology: affixes located in the middle of words.)

Such affix and letter sequence pairing results can clearly be useful for English speakers learning Spanish (and vice versa), for remembering words by associating them to known ones, for avoidance of spelling mistakes, and for analyzing previously unseen words.

Evaluation. An unsupervised learning model can be evaluated on the strength of the phenomena that it discovers, on its predictive power for unseen data, or by comparing its data analysis results with results obtained using other means. We have performed all three evaluations.

For evaluating the discovered phenomena, a repository of known phenomena is needed. The only such repository of which we are aware are language learning texts. Unfortunately, the phenomena these present are limited to the few most conspicuous pairs (e.g., -ly:-mente, -ity:-idad, ph:f), all of which are easily discovered by our model. The next best thing are studies that present data of a single language. We took the affix information given in a recent, highly detailed, corpus based English grammar (Biber99), and compared it manually to ours. Of the 35 most productive affixes, our model finds 27. Careful study of the word pair list showed that the remaining 8 (-ment, -ship, -age, -ful, -less, -en, dis-, mis-) indeed do not map to Spanish ones frequently. Note that some of those are indeed extremely frequent inside English yet do not correspond significantly with any Spanish affix.

As a second test, we took a comprehensive English-Spanish dictionary (Collins), selected 10 pages at random (out of 680), studied them, and listed the prominent word form phenomena (85). All but one (the verbal suffix in seduce:seducir) were found by our model.

The numbers reported above for the two tests are recall numbers. To evaluate affix precision, we have manually graded the top 100 affix pairs (as sorted at the end of stage 2 of the algorithm.) 8 of those were clearly not affixes; however, 3 of the 8 (-t:-te, –t:-to, -ve:-vo) were important phonological phenomena that should indeed appear in our final model. Of the remaining 92, 15 were valid but 'duplicates' in the sense of being substrings of other affixes (e.g., -ly:-mente, -ly:-emente.) In the next 50 pairs, only 6 were clearly not affixes. Note that by their very definition, we should not expect the number of frequent derivational affixes to be very large, so there is not much point in looking further down the list. Nonetheless, inspection of the rest of the list reveals that it is not dominated by noise but by duplicates, with many specialized, less frequent affixes (e.g., -graphy:-grafia) being discovered.

Regarding letter sequences, precision was very high: of the 38 different pairs discovered, only one (hr:r) was not regular, and there were 11 duplicates. Recall was impressive, but harder to verify due to the lack of standards. We found only one (not very frequent) pair that was not discovered (-sp:-esp).

To evaluate the model on its data analysis capability, we took out 100 word pairs at random, trained the model without them, analyzed them using the final cost function, and compared with prominent phenomena noted manually (again, we had to grade manually due to the lack of a gold standard.) The model identified those prominent phenomena (including a total lack thereof) in 91 of the pairs. Notable failures included the pairs superscribe : sobrescribir and coded : codificado, where none of the prefixes and suffixes were identified. Some successful examples are listed below (affixes are denoted by [], sequences by <>, and insert by _: or :_):

installation : instalacion. <ll:l>, [ation:acion]
volution : circonvolucion. _:c, _:i, _:r, _:c, _:o, _:n, [tion:cion]
intelligibility : inteligibilidad. [in:in], <ll:l>, [ity:idad]
sapper : zapador. <s:z>, <pp:p>, [er:ador]
harpist : arpista. <h:_>, [ist:ista]
pathologist : patologo. <th:t>, [ist:o]
elongate : prolongar. [te:r]
industrialize: industrializar. [in:in], <ial>, [e:ar]
demographic : demografico. <ph:f>, [ic:ico]
gynecological :ginecologico. <yn:in>, [ical:ico]
peeled : pelado. [ed:ado]

The third and final evaluation method is to compare the model's results with results obtained using other means. We are not aware of any data bank in which cross-language affix or letter sequence correspondences are explicitly tagged, so we had used a relatively simple algorithm as a baseline: We invoked the squares method for each language independently, ending up with affix candidates. For every word pair E:S, if E contains an affix candidate C and S contains an affix candidate D, we increment the count of the candidate affix pair C:D. Finally, we sort the candidates according to their count.

Baseline recall is obviously as good as in our algorithm (it produces a superset), but precision is so bad so as to render the baseline method useless: out of the first 100, only 19 were affixes, the rest being made up of noise and badly segmented 'duplicates'.

In summary, the results are good, but gold standards are needed for a more consistent evaluation of different cross-language word form algorithms. Results for the other language pairs were overall good as well.

6 Discussion

We have introduced the problem of cross-language modeling of word forms, presented an algorithm for addressing affixal morphology and letter sequences, and described good results on English-Spanish dictionary word pairs.

Natural directions for future work on the model include: (1) test the algorithm on more language pairs, including languages utilizing non-Latin alphabets; (2) modify the input model to assume that single language affixes are known; (3) address additional morphological operators, such as templatic morphology; (4) address phonology directly instead of indirectly; (5) use pairs acquired from a parallel corpus rather than a dictionary, to address inflectional morphology and to see how the algorithm performs with more noisy data; (6) extend the algorithm to other types of writing systems; (7) examine more sophisticated affix discovery algorithms, such as (Goldsmith01); and (8) improve the evaluation methodology.

There are many possible applications of the model: (1) for statistical machine translation; (2) for computational historical linguistics; (3) for CLIR back-transliteration; (4) for constructing learning materials and word memorization methods in second language education; and (5) for improving word form learning algorithms inside a single language.

The length and diversity of the lists above provide an indication of the benefit and importance of cross-language word form modeling in computational linguistics and its application areas.

References

Biber Douglas, 1999. Longman Grammar of Spoken and Written English. (Pages 320, 399, 530, 539.)

Bilac Slaven, Tanaka Hozumi, 2004. A Hybrid Back-Transliteration System for Japanese. COLING 2004.

Brill Eric, Moore Robert, 2000. An Improved Error Model for Noisy Channel Spelling Correction. ACL 2000.

Covington Michael A, 1996. An Algorithm to Align Words for Historical Comparison. Comput. Ling., 22(4):481—496.

Creutz Mathias, Lugas Krista, 2004. Induction of a Simple Morphology for Highly-Inflecting Languages. ACL 2004 Workshop on Comput. Phonology and Morphology.

Freelang, 2004. http: // www.freelang.net / dictionary / spanish.html.

Goldsmith John. 2001. Unsupervised Learning of the Morphology of a Natural Language. Comput. Ling. 153-189 (also see an unpublished 2004 document at http://humanities.uchicago.edu/faculty/goldsmith.)

Gusfield, Dan, 1997. Algorithms on Strings, Trees, and Sequences. Cambridge University Press.

Knight Kevin, Graehl Jonathan, 1998. Machine Transliteration. Comput. Ling. 24(4):599—612.

Kondrak Grzegorz, 2003a. Phonetic Alignment and Similarity. Comput. & the Humanities 37:273—291.

Kondrak Grzegorz, 2003b. Identifying Complex Sound Correspondences in Bilingual Wordlists.. Comput. Ling. & Intelligent Text Processing (CICLing 2003).

Kondrak Grzegorz, Marcu Daniel, Knight Kevin, 2003. Cognates Can Improve Statistical Translation Models. Human Language Technology (HLT) 2003.

Li Haizhou et al, 2004. A Joint Source-Channel Model for Machine Transliteration. ACL 2004.

Lin Wei-Hao, Chen Hsin-Hsi, 2002. Backward Machine Transliteration by Learning Phonetic Similarity. CoNLL 2002.

Mackay Wesley, Kondrak Grzegorz, 2005. Computing Word Similarity and Identifying Cognates with Pair Hidden Markov Models. CoNLL 2005.

Matlin Margaret W., 2002. Cognition, 6th ed. John Wiley & Sons.

Medina Urrea Alfonso, 2000. Automatic Discovery of Affixes by Means of a Corpus: A Catalog of Spanish Affixes. J. of Quantitative Linguistics 7(3):97 – 114.

Melamed Dan, 1997. Automatic Discovery of Non-Compositional Compounds in Parallel Data. EMNLP 1997.

Mueller Karin, 2005. Revealing Phonological Similarities between Related Languages from Automatically Generated Parallel Corpora. ACL '05 Workshop on Building and Using Parallel Texts.

Niessen Sonja, Ney Hermann, 2000. Improving SMT Quality with Morph-syntactic analysis. COLING 2000.

Ristad Eric Sven, Yianilos Peter, 1998. Learning String Edit Distance. IEEE PAMI, 20(5):522—532.

Schulz Stefan, et al 2004. Cognate Mapping. COLING 2004.

Wicentowsky Richard, 2004. Multilingual Noise-Robust Supervised Morphological Analysis using the WordFrame Model. ACL 2004 Workshop on Comput. Phonology and Morphology.

Eng.	Span.	Wit.	Squ.	Example
-tion	-	623	309	reformation:reforma
-e	-ar	461	1182	convene:convocar
-tion	-cion	434	3770	vibration:vibracion
co-	co-	363	95	coexistence:coexistencia
-ness	-	352	128	persuasiveness:persuasiva
-ation	-acion	333	4854	formulation:formulacion
in-	In-	332	1294	inapt:inepto
re-	Re-	312	194	recreative:recreativo
-ed	-ado	289	102	abridged:abreviado
-ic	-ico	274	3192	strategic:estrategico
-ly	-mente	269	207	aggressively:agresivamente
-y	-ia	251	2086	agronomy:agronomia
-ble	-ble	238	153	incredible:increible
-al	-al	233	440	genital:genital
-ity	-idad	208	687	stability:estabilidad
-te	-r	206	3603	tabulate:tabular
-er	-o	203	166	biographer:biografo
-al	-o	186	2728	practical:practico
de-	de-	174	68	deformation:deformacion
-ate	-ar	170	3593	manipulate:manipular
-ous	-o	154	59	analogous:analogo
con-	con-	153	53	conceivable:concebible
-ism	-ismo	147	2173	tourism:turismo
un-	In-	134	164	undistinguishable:indistinto
-er	-ador	134	95	progammer:programador
-nt	-nte	120	514	tolerant:tolerante
-ical	-ico	111	3185	lyrical:lirico
-ist	-ista	111	1691	tourist:turista
-ize	-izar	90	974	privatize:privatizar
-ce	-cia	87	445	belligerence:beligerancia
-tive	-tivo	70	249	superlative:superlativo

Table 1: Some affix pairs discovered.

Eng.	Span.	Example
ph	f	aphoristic:aforistico
th	t	lithography:litografia
ll	l	collaboration:colaboracion
tion	cion	unconditional:incodicional
st-	est-	stylist:estilista
tia	cia	unnegotiable:innegociable

Table 2: Some letter sequence pairs discovered.

Improving Name Discrimination: A Language Salad Approach

Ted Pedersen and **Anagha Kulkarni**
Department of Computer Science
University of Minnesota, Duluth
Duluth, MN 55812 USA
{tpederse,kulka020}@d.umn.edu

Roxana Angheluta
Attentio SA
B-1030 Brussels, Belgium
roxana@attentio.com

Zornitsa Kozareva
Dept. de Lenguajes y Sistemas Informáticos
University of Alicante
03080 Alicante, Spain
zkozareva@dlsi.ua.es

Thamar Solorio
Department of Computer Science
University of Texas at El Paso
El Paso, TX 79902 USA
tsolorio@utep.edu

Abstract

This paper describes a method of discriminating ambiguous names that relies upon features found in corpora of a more abundant language. In particular, we discriminate ambiguous names in Bulgarian, Romanian, and Spanish corpora using information derived from much larger quantities of English data. We also mix together occurrences of the ambiguous name found in English with the occurrences of the name in the language in which we are trying to discriminate. We refer to this as a language salad, and find that it often results in even better performance than when only using English or the language itself as the source of information for discrimination.

1 Introduction

Name ambiguity is a problem that is increasing in complexity and scope as online information sources grow and expand their coverage. Like words, names are often ambiguous and can refer to multiple underlying entities or concepts. Web searches for names can often return results associated with multiple people or organizations in a disorganized and unclear fashion. For example, the top 10 results of a Google search for *George Miller* includes a mixture of entries for two different entities, one a psychology professor from Princeton University and the other the director of the film *Mad Max*.[1]

Name discrimination takes some number of contexts that include an ambiguous name, and divides them into groups or clusters, where the contexts in each cluster should ideally refer to the same underlying entity (and each cluster should refer to a different entity). Thus, if we are given 10,000 contexts that include the name *John Smith*, we would want to divide those contexts into clusters corresponding to each of the different underlying entities that share that name.

We have developed an unsupervised method of name discrimination (Pedersen et al., 2005). We have shown the method to be language independent (Pedersen et al., 2006), which is to say we can apply it to English contexts as easily as we can apply it to Romanian or French. However, we have observed that there are situations where the number of contexts in which an ambiguous name occurs is relatively small, perhaps because the name itself is unusual, or because the quantity of data available for language is limited in general. These problems of scarcity can make it difficult to apply these methods and discriminate ambiguous names, especially in languages with fewer online resources.

This paper presents a method of name discrimination is based on using a larger number of contexts in English that include an ambiguous name, and applying information derived from these contexts to the discrimination of that name in another language, where there are many fewer contexts. We also show that mixing English contexts with the contexts to be discriminated can result in a performance improvement over only using the English or the original contexts alone.

2 Discrimination by Clustering Contexts

Our method of name discrimination is described in more detail in (Pedersen et al., 2005), but in general is based on an unsupervised approach to word sense discrimination introduced by (Purandare and

[1] Search conducted January 4, 2006.

Pedersen, 2004), which builds upon earlier work in word sense discrimination, including (Schütze, 1998) and (Pedersen and Bruce, 1997).

Our method treats each occurrence of an ambiguous name as a context that is to be clustered with other contexts that also include the same name. In this paper, each context consists of about 50 words, where the ambiguous name is generally in the middle of the context. The goal is to cluster similar contexts together, based on the presumption that the occurrences of a name that appear in similar contexts will refer to the same underlying entity. This approach is motivated by both the *distributional hypothesis* (Harris, 1968) and the *strong contextual hypothesis* (Miller and Charles, 1991).

2.1 Feature Selection

The contexts to be clustered are represented by lexical features which may be selected from either the contexts being clustered, or from a separate corpus. In this paper we use both approaches. We cluster the contexts based on features identified in those very same contexts, and we also cluster the contexts based on features identified in a separate set of data (in this case English). We explore the use of a mixed feature selection strategy where we identify features both from the data to be clustered and the separate corpus of English text. Thus, our *feature selection data* may come from one of three sources: the contexts to be clustered (which we will refer to as the *evaluation contexts*), English contexts which include the same name but are not to be clustered, and the combination of these two (our so-called Language Salad or Mix).

The lexical features we employ are bigrams, that is consecutive words that occur together in the corpora from which we are identifying features. In this work we identify bigram features using Pointwise Mutual Information (PMI). This is defined as the log of the ratio of the observed frequency with which the two words occur together in the feature selection data, to the expected number of times the two words would occur together in a corpus if they were independent. This expected value is estimated simply by taking the product of the number of times the two words occur individually, and dividing this by the total number of bigrams in the feature selection data. Thus, larger values of PMI indicate that the observed frequency of the bigram is greater than would be expected if the two words were independent.

In these experiments we take the top 500 ranked bigrams that occur five or more times in the feature selection data. We also exclude any bigram from consideration that is made up of one or two stop words, which are high frequency function words that have been specified in a manually created list. Note that with smaller numbers of contexts (usually 200 or fewer), we lower the frequency threshold to two or more.

In general PMI is known to have a bias towards pairs of words (bigrams) that occur a small number of times and only with each other. In this work that is a desirable quality, since that will tend to identify pairs of words that are very strongly associated with each other and also provide unique discriminating information.

2.2 Context Representation

Once the bigram features have been identified, then the contexts to be clustered are represented using *second order co-occurrences* that are derived from those bigrams. In general a second order co-occurrence is a pair of words that may not occur with each other, but that both occur frequently with a third word. For example, *garden* and *fire* may not occur together often, but both commonly occur with *hose*. Thus, *garden hose* and *fire hose* represent first order co–occurrences, and *garden* and *fire* represent a second order co–occurrence.

The process of creating the second order representation has several steps. First, the bigram features identified by PMI (the top ranked 500 bigrams that have occurred 5 or more times in the feature selection data) are used to create a word by word co–occurrence matrix. The first word in each bigram represents a row in the matrix, and the second word in each bigram represents a column. The cells in the matrix contain the PMI scores. Note that this matrix is not symmetric, and that there are many words that only occur in either a row or a column (and not both) because they tend to occur as the first or second word in a bigram. For example, *President* might tend to be a first word in a bigram (e.g., *President Clinton, President Putin*), whereas last names will tend to be the second word.

Once the co–occurrence matrix is created, then the contexts to be clustered can be represented. Each word in the context is checked to see if it has a corresponding row (i.e., vector) in the co–occurrence matrix. If it does, that word is replaced in the context by the row from the matrix, so that the word in the context is now represented by the vector of words with which it occurred in the feature selection data. If a word does not have a corresponding entry in the co–occurrence matrix, then it is simply removed from the context. After all the words in the context are checked, then all of the vectors that are selected are averaged together to create a vector representation of the context.

Then these contexts are clustered into a pre–specified number of clusters using the k–means algorithm. Note that we are currently developing methods to automatically select the number of clusters in the data (e.g., (Pedersen and Kulkarni, 2006)), although we have not yet applied them to this particular work.

3 The Language Salad

In this paper, we explore the creation of a second order representation for a set of evaluation contexts using three different sets of feature selection data. The co–occurrence matrix may be derived from the evaluation contexts themselves, or from a separate set of contexts in a different language, or from the combination of these two (the Salad or Mix).

For example, suppose we have 100 Romanian evaluation contexts that include an ambiguous name, and that same name also occurs 10,000 times in an English language corpus.[2] Our goal is to cluster the 100 Romanian contexts, which contain all the information that we have about the name in Romanian. While we could derive a second order representation of the contexts, the resulting co–occurrence matrix would likely be very small and sparse, and insufficient for making good discrimination decisions. We could instead rely on first order features, that is look for frequent words or bigrams that occur in the evaluation contexts, and try and find evaluation contexts that share some of the same words or phrases, and cluster them based on this type of information. However, again, the small number of contexts available would likely result in very sparse representations for the contexts, and unreliable clustering results.

Thus, our method is to derive a co–occurrence matrix from a language for which we have many occurrences of the ambiguous name, and then use that co–occurrence matrix to represent the evaluation contexts. This relies on the fact that the evaluation contexts will contain at least a few names or words that are also used in the larger corpus (in this case English). In general, we have found that while this is not always true, it is often the case.

We have also experimented with combining the English contexts with the evaluation contexts, and building a co–occurrence matrix based on this combined or mixed collection of contexts. This is the language salad that we refer to, a mixture of contexts in two different languages that are used to derive a representation of the evaluation contexts.

[2]We assume that the names either have the same spelling in both languages, or that translations are readily available.

4 Experimental Data

We use data in four languages in these experiments, Bulgarian, English, Romanian, and Spanish.

4.1 Raw Corpora

The Romanian data comes from the 2004 archives of the newspaper Adevarul (The Truth)[3]. This is a daily newspaper that is among the most popular in Romania. While Romanian normally has diacritical markings, this particular newspaper does not include those in their online edition, so the alphabet used was the same as English.

The Bulgarian data is from the Sega 2002 news corpus, which was originally prepared for the CLEF competition.[4] This is a corpus of news articles from the Newspaper Sega[5], which is based in Sofia, Bulgaria. The Bulgarian text was transliterated (phonetically) from Cyrillic to the Roman alphabet. Thus, the alphabet used was the same as English, although the phonetic transliteration leads to fewer cognates and borrowed English words that are spelled exactly the same as in English text.

The Spanish corpora comes from the Spanish news agency EFE from the year 1994 and 1995. This collection was used in the Question Answering Track at CLEF-2003, and also for CLEF-2005. This text is represented in Latin-1, and includes the usual accents that appear in Spanish.

The English data comes from the GigaWord corpus (2nd edition) that is distributed by the Linguistic Data Consortium. This consists of more

[3]http://www.adevarulonline.ro/arhiva

[4]http://www.clef-campaign.org

[5]http://www.segabg.com

than 2 billion words of newspaper text that comes from five different news sources between the years 1994 and 2004. In fact, we subdivide the English data into three different corpora, where one is from 2004, another from 2002, and the third from 1994-95, so that for each of the evaluation languages (Bulgarian, Spanish, and Romanian) we have an English corpus from the same time period.

4.2 Evaluation Contexts

Our experimental data consists of evaluation contexts derived from the Bulgarian, Romanian, and Spanish corpora mentioned above. We also have English corpora that includes the same ambiguous names as found in the evaluation contexts.

In order to quickly generate a large volume of experimental data, we created evaluation contexts from the corpora for each of our four languages by conflating together pairs of well known names or places, and that are generally not highly ambiguous (although some might be rather general). For example, one of the pairs of names we conflate is *George Bush* and *Tony Blair*. To do that, every occurrence of both of these names is converted to an ambiguous form (GB_TB, for example), and the discrimination task is to cluster these contexts such that their original and correct name is re–discovered. We retain a record of the original name for each occurrence, so as to evaluate the results of our method. Of course we do not use this information anywhere in the process outside of evaluation.

The following pairs of names were conflated in all four of the languages: George Bush-Tony Blair, Mexico-India, USA-Paris, Ronaldo-David Beckham (2002 and 2004), Diego Maradona-Roberto Baggio (1994-95 only), and NATO-USA. Note that some of these names have different spellings in some of our languages, so we look for and conflate the native spelling of the names in the different language corpora. These pairs were selected because they occur in all four of our languages, and they represent name distinctions that are commonly of interest, that is they represent ambiguity in names of people and places. With these pairs we are also following (Nakov and Hearst, 2003) who suggest that if one is introducing ambiguity by creating *pseudo—words* or conflating names, then these words should be related in some way (in order to avoid the creation of very sharp or obvious sense distinctions).

4.3 Discussion

For each of the three evaluation languages (Bulgarian, Romanian, and Spanish) we have contexts for five different name conflate pairs that we wish to discriminate. We have corresponding English contexts for each evaluation language, where the dates of both are approximately the same. This temporal consistency between the evaluation language and English is important because the contexts in which a name is used may change over time. In 1994, for example, Tony Blair was not yet Prime Minister of England (he became PM in 1997), and references to George Bush most likely refer to the US President who served from 1988 until 1992, rather than the current US President (who began his term in office in 2001). In 1994 the current (as of 2006) US President had just been elected governor of Texas, and was not yet a national figure. This points out that George Bush is an example of an ambiguous name, but our observation has been that in the 2002 and 2004 data (Romanian and Bulgarian) nearly all occurrences are associated with the current president, and that most of the occurrences in 1994-95 (Spanish) refer to the former US President. This illustrates an important point: it is necessary to consider the perspective represented by the different corpora. There is little reason to expect that news articles from Spain in 1994 and 1995 would focus much attention on the newly elected governor of Texas in the United States.

Tables 1, 2, and 3 show the number of contexts that have been collected for each name conflate pair. For example, in Table 1 we see that there are 746 Bulgarian contexts that refer to either Mexico or India, and that of these 51.47% truly refer to Mexico, and 48.53% to India. There are 149,432 English contexts that mention Mexico or India, and the Mix value shown is simply the sum of the number of Bulgarian and English contexts.

In general these tables show that the English contexts are much larger in number, however, there are a few exceptions with the Spanish data. This is because the EFE corpus is relatively large as compared to the Bulgarian and Romanian corpora, and provides frequency counts that are in some cases comparable to those in the English corpus.

5 Experimental Methodology

For each of the three evaluation languages (Bulgarian, Romanian, Spanish) there are five name conflate pairs. The same name conflate pairs are used for all three languages, except for Diego Maradona-Roberto Baggio which is only used with Spanish, and Ronaldo-David Beckham, which is only used with Bulgarian and Romanian. This is due to the fact that in 1994-95 (the era of the Spanish data) neither Ronaldo nor David Beckham were as famous as they later became, so they were mentioned somewhat less often than in the 2002 and 2004 corpora. The other four name conflate pairs are used in all of the languages.

For each name conflate pair we create a second order representation using three different sources of features selection data: the evaluation contexts themselves, the corresponding English contexts, and then the mix of the evaluation contexts and the English contexts (the Mix). The objective of these experiments is to determine which of these sources of feature selection data results in the highest F-Measure, which is the harmonic mean of the precision and recall of an experiment.

The precision of each experiment is the number of evaluation contexts clustered correctly, divided by the number of contexts that are clustered. The clustering algorithm may choose not to assign every context to a cluster, which is why that denominator may not be the same as the number of evaluation contexts. The recall of each experiment is the the number of correctly clustered evaluation contexts divided by the total number of evaluation contexts. Note that for each of the three variations for each name conflate pair experiment exactly the same evaluation language contexts are being discriminated, all that is changing in each experiment is the source of the feature selection data. Thus the F-measures for a name conflate pair in a particular language can be compared directly. Note however that the F-measures across languages are harder to compare directly, since different evaluation contexts are used, and different English contexts are used as well.

There is a simple baseline that can be used as a point of comparison, and that is to place all of the contexts for each name conflate pair into one cluster, and say that there is no ambiguity. If that is done, then the resulting F-Measure will be equal to the majority percentage of the true underlying entity as shown in Tables 1, 2, and 3. For example, for Bulgarian, if the 746 Bulgarian contexts for Mexico and India are all put into the same cluster, the resulting F-Measure would be 51.47%, because we would simply assign all the contexts in the cluster to the more common of the two entities, which is Mexico in this case.

6 Experimental Results

Tables 1, 2, and 3 show the results for our experiments, language by language. Each table shows the results for the 15 experiments done for each language: five name conflate pairs, each with three different sources of feature selection data. The row labeled with the name of the evaluation language reports the F-Measure for the evaluation contexts (whose number of occurrences is shown in the far right column) when the feature selection data is the evaluation contexts themselves. The rows labeled English and Mix report the F-Measures obtained for the evaluation contexts when the feature selection data is the English contexts, or the Mix of the English and evaluation contexts.

6.1 Bulgarian Results

The Bulgarian results are shown in Table 1. Note that the number of contexts for English is considerably larger than for Bulgarian for all five name conflate pairs. The Bulgarian and English data came from 2002 news reports.

The Mix of feature selection data results in the best performance for three of the five name conflate pairs: George Bush - Tony Blair, Ronaldo - David Beckham, and NATO - USA. For remaining two name conflate pairs, just using the Bulgarian evaluation contexts results in the highest F-Measure (Mexico-India, USA-Paris).

We believe that this may be partially due to the fact that the two cases where Bulgarian leads to the best results are for very general or generic underlying entities: Mexico and India, and then the USA and Paris. In both cases, contexts that mention these entities could be discussing a wide range of topics, and the larger volumes of English data may simply overwhelm the process with a huge number of second order features. In addition, it may be that the English and Bulgarian corpora contain different content that reflects the different interests of the original readership of this text. For example, news that is reported about India might be rather different in the United States (the source of most

Table 1: Bulgarian Results (2002): Feature Selection Data, F-Measure, and Number of Contexts

George Bush (73.43) - Tony Blair (26.57)		
Mix	68.37	11,570
Bulgarian	55.78	651
English	36.15	10,919
Mexico (51.47) - India (48.53)		
Bulgarian	70.97	746
Mix	55.01	150,178
English	48.15	149,432
USA (79.53) - Paris (20.47)		
Bulgarian	58.67	3,283
Mix	51.68	56,044
English	49.66	52,761
Ronaldo (61.25) - David Beckham (38.75)		
Mix	64.88	8,649
Bulgarian	52.75	320
English	48.11	8,329
NATO (87.37) - USA (12.63)		
Mix	75.44	54,193
Bulgarian	65.92	3,770
English	60.44	50,423

Table 2: Romanian Results (2004): Feature Selection Data, F-Measure, and Number of Contexts

Tony Blair (72.00) - George Bush (28.00)		
English	64.23	11,616
Mix	54.31	11,816
Romanian	50.75	200
India (53.66) - Mexico (46.34)		
Romanian	50.93	82
English	47.30	88,247
Mix	42.55	88,329
USA (60.29) - Paris (39.71)		
English	59.05	45,346
Romanian	58.76	700
Mix	57.91	46,046
David Beckham (55.56) - Ronaldo (44.44)		
Mix	81.00	4,365
English	70.85	4,203
Romanian	52.47	162
NATO (58.05) - USA (41.95)		
Mix	60.48	43,508
Romanian	51.20	1,168
English	38.91	42,340

of the English data) than in Bulgaria. Thus, the use of the English corpora might not have been as helpful in those cases where the names to be discriminated are more global figures. For example, Tony Blair and George Bush are probably in the news in the USA and Bulgaria for many of the same reasons, thus the underlying content is more comparable than that of the more general entities (like Mexico and India) that might have much different content associated with them.

We observed that Bulgarian tends to have fewer cognates or shared names with English than do Romanian and English. This is due to the fact that the Bulgarian text is transliterated. This may account for the fact that the English-only results for Bulgarian are very poor, and it is only in combination with the Bulgarian contexts that the English contexts show any positive effect. This suggests that there are only a few words in the Bulgarian contexts that also occur in English, but those that do have a positive impact on clustering performance.

6.2 Romanian Results

The Romanian results are shown in Table 2. The Romanian and English contexts come from 2004.

The Mix of Romanian and English contexts for feature selection results in improvements for two of the five pairs (David Beckham - Ronaldo, and NATO - USA). The use of English contexts only provides the best results for two other pairs (Tony Blair - George Bush, and USA - Paris, although in the latter case the difference in the F-Measures that result from the three sources of data is minimal). There is one case (Mexico-India) where using the Romanian contexts as feature selection data results in a slightly better F-measure than when using English contexts.

The improvement that the Mix shows for David Beckham-Ronaldo is significant, and is perhaps due to fact that in both English and Romanian text, the content about Beckham and Ronaldo is similar, making it more likely that the mix of English and Romanian contexts will be helpful. However, it is also true that the Mix results in a significant improvement for NATO-USA, and it seems likely that the local perspective in Romania and the USA would be somewhat different on these two entities. However, NATO-USA has a relatively large number of contexts in Romanian as well as English, so perhaps the difference in perspective had less of an impact in those cases where the number of Ro-

Table 3: Spanish Results (1994-95): Feature Selection Data, F-Measure, and Number of Contexts

George Bush (75.58) - Tony Blair (24.42)		
Mix	78.59	2,353
Spanish	64.45	1,163
English	54.29	1,190
D. Maradona (51.55) - R. Baggio (48.45)		
English	67.65	1,588
Mix	61.35	3,594
Spanish	60.70	2,006
India (92.34) - Mexico (7.66)		
English	72.76	19,540
Spanish	66.57	2,377
Mix	61.54	21,917
USA (62.30) - Paris (37.70)		
Spanish	69.31	1,000
English	64.30	17,344
Mix	59.40	18,344
NATO (63.86) - USA (36.14)		
Spanish	62.04	2,172
Mix	58.47	27,426
English	56.00	25,254

manian contexts is much smaller (as is the case for Beckham and Ronaldo).

6.3 Spanish Results

The Spanish results are shown in Table 3. The Spanish and English contexts come from 1994-1995, which puts them in a slightly different historical era than the Bulgarian and Romanian corpora.

Due to this temporal difference, we used Diego Maradona and Roberto Baggio as a conflated pair, rather than David Beckham and Ronaldo, who were much younger and somewhat less famous at that time. Also, Ronaldo is a highly ambiguous name in Spanish, as it is a very common first name. This is true in English text as well, although casual inspection of the English text from 2002 and 2004 (where the Ronaldo-Beckham pair was included experimentally) reveals that Ronaldo the soccer player tends to occur more so than any other single entity named Ronaldo, so while there is a bit more noise for Ronaldo, there is not really a significant ambiguity.

For the Spanish results we only note one pair (George Bush - Tony Blair) where the Mix of English and Spanish results in the best performance. This again suggests that the perspective of the Spanish and English corpora were similar with respect to these entities, and their combination was helpful. In two other cases (Maradona-Baggio, India-Mexico) English only contexts achieve the highest F-Measure, and then in the two remaining cases (USA-Paris, NATO-USA) the Spanish contexts are the best source of features.

Note that for Spanish we have reasonably large numbers of contexts (as compared to Bulgarian and Romanian). Given that, it is especially interesting that English-only contexts are the most effective in two of five cases. This suggests that this approach may have merit even when the evaluation language does not suffer from problems of extreme scarcity. It may simply be that the information in the English corpora provides more discriminating information than does the Spanish, and that it is somewhat different in content than the Spanish, otherwise we would expect the Mix of English and Spanish contexts to do better than being most accurate for just one of five cases.

7 Discussion

Of the 15 name conflate experiments (five pairs, three languages), in only five cases did the use of the evaluation contexts as a source of feature selection data result in better F-Measure scores than did either using the English contexts alone or as a Mix with the evaluation language contexts. Thus, we conclude that there is a clear benefit to using feature selection data that comes from a different language than the one for which discrimination is being performed.

We believe that this is due to the volume of the English data, as well as to the nature of the name discrimination task. For example, a person is often best described or identified by observing the people he or she tends to associate with, or the places he or she visits, or the companies with which he or she does business. If we observe that *George Miller* and *Mel Gibson* occur together, then it seems we can safely infer that *George Miller* the movie director is being referred to, rather than *George Miller* the psychologist and father of WordNet.

This argument might suggest that first order co–occurrences would be sufficient to discriminate among the names. That is, simply group the evaluation contexts based on the features that occur within them, and essentially cluster evaluation contexts based on the number of features they have in common with other evaluation contexts. In fact, results on word sense discrimination (Purandare and Pedersen, 2004) suggest that first order representations are more effective with larger number of context than second order methods. However, we see examples in these results that suggests this may not always be the case. In the Bulgarian results, the largest number of Bulgarian contexts are for NATO-USA, but the Mix performs quite a bit better than Bulgarian only. In the case of Romanian, again NATO-USA has the largest number of contexts, but the Mix still does better than Romanian only. And in Spanish, Mexico-India has the largest number of contexts and English-only does better. Thus, even in cases where we have an abundant number of evaluation contexts, the indirect nature of the second order representation provides some added benefit.

We believe that the perspective of the news organizations providing the corpora certainly has an impact on the results. For example, in Romanian, the news about David Beckham and Ronaldo is probably much the same as in the United States. These are international figures that are both external to countries where the news originates, and there is no reason to suppose there would be a unique local perspective represented by any of the news sources. The only difference among them might be in the number of contexts available. In this situation, the addition of the English contexts may provide enough additional information to improve discrimination performance in another language.

For example, in the 162 Romanian contexts for Ronaldo-Beckham, there is one occurrence of *Posh*, which was the stage name of Beckham's wife Victoria. This is below our frequency cutoff threshold for feature selection, so it would be discarded when using Romanian–only contexts. However, in the English contexts Posh is mentioned 6 times, and is included as a feature. Thus, the one occurrence of *Posh* in the Romanian corpus can be well represented by information found in the English contexts, thus allowing that Romanian context to be correctly discriminated.

8 Conclusions

This paper shows that a method of name discrimination based on second order context representations can take advantage of English contexts, and the mix of English and evaluation contexts, in order to perform more accurate name discrimination.

9 Acknowledgments

This research is supported by a National Science Foundation Faculty Early CAREER Development Award (#0092784). All of the experiments in this paper were carried out with version 0.71 SenseClusters package, which is freely available from http://senseclusters.sourceforge.net.

References

Z. Harris. 1968. *Mathematical Structures of Language*. Wiley, New York.

G.A. Miller and W.G. Charles. 1991. Contextual correlates of semantic similarity. *Language and Cognitive Processes*, 6(1):1–28.

P. Nakov and M. Hearst. 2003. Category-based pseudowords. In *Companion Volume to the Proceedings of HLT-NAACL 2003 - Short Papers*, pages 67–69, Edmonton, Alberta, Canada, May 27 - June 1.

T. Pedersen and R. Bruce. 1997. Distinguishing word senses in untagged text. In *Proceedings of the Second Conference on Empirical Methods in Natural Language Processing*, pages 197–207, Providence, RI, August.

T. Pedersen and A. Kulkarni. 2006. Selecting the ŕightńumber of senses based on clustering criterion functions. In *Proceedings of the Posters and Demo Program of the Eleventh Conference of the European Chapter of the Association for Computational Linguistics*, Trento, Italy, April.

T. Pedersen, A. Purandare, and A. Kulkarni. 2005. Name discrimination by clustering similar contexts. In *Proceedings of the Sixth International Conference on Intelligent Text Processing and Computational Linguistics*, pages 220–231, Mexico City, February.

T. Pedersen, A. Kulkarni, R. Angheluta, Z. Kozareva, and T. Solorio. 2006. An unsupervised language independent method of name discrimination using second order co-occurrence features. In *Proceedings of the Seventh International Conference on Intelligent Text Processing and Computational Linguistics*, pages 208–222, Mexico City, February.

A. Purandare and T. Pedersen. 2004. Word sense discrimination by clustering contexts in vector and similarity spaces. In *Proceedings of the Conference on Computational Natural Language Learning*, pages 41–48, Boston, MA.

H. Schütze. 1998. Automatic word sense discrimination. *Computational Linguistics*, 24(1):97–123.

Tagging Portuguese with a Spanish Tagger Using Cognates

Jirka Hana
Department of Linguistics
The Ohio State University
hana.1@osu.edu

Anna Feldman
Department of Linguistics
The Ohio State University
afeldman@ling.osu.edu

Chris Brew
Department of Linguistics
The Ohio State University
cbrew@acm.org

Luiz Amaral
Department of Spanish and Portuguese
The Ohio State University
amaral.1@osu.edu

Abstract

We describe a knowledge and resource light system for an automatic morphological analysis and tagging of Brazilian Portuguese.[1] We avoid the use of labor intensive resources; particularly, large annotated corpora and lexicons. Instead, we use (i) an annotated corpus of Peninsular Spanish, a language related to Portuguese, (ii) an unannotated corpus of Portuguese, (iii) a description of Portuguese morphology on the level of a basic grammar book. We extend the similar work that we have done (Hana et al., 2004; Feldman et al., 2006) by proposing an alternative algorithm for cognate transfer that effectively projects the Spanish emission probabilities into Portuguese. Our experiments use minimal new human effort and show 21% error reduction over even emissions on a fine-grained tagset.

1 Introduction

Part of speech (POS) tagging is an important step in natural language processing. Corpora that have been POS-tagged are very useful both for linguistic research, e.g. finding instances or frequencies of particular constructions (Meurers, 2004) and for further computational processing, such as syntactic parsing, speech recognition, stemming, word-sense disambiguation. *Morphological tagging* is the process of assigning POS, case, number, gender and other morphological information to each word in a corpus. Despite the importance of morphological tagging, there are many languages that lack annotated resources of this kind, mainly due to the lack of training corpora which are usually required for applying standard statistical taggers.

Applications of taggers include syntactic parsing, stemming, text-to-speech synthesis, word-sense disambiguation, information extraction. For some of these getting all the tags right is inessential, e.g. the input to noun phrase chunking does not necessarily require high accuracy fine-grained tag resolution.

Cross-language information transfer is not new; however, most of the existing work relies on parallel corpora (e.g. Hwa et al., 2004; Yarowsky and Ngai, 2001) which are difficult to find, especially for lesser studied languages. In this paper, we describe a cross-language method that requires neither training data of the target language nor bilingual lexicons or parallel corpora. We report the results of the experiments done on Brazilian Portuguese and Peninsular Spanish, however, our system is not tied to these particular languages. The method is easily portable to other (inflected) languages. Our method assumes that an annotated corpus exists for the source language (here, Spanish) and that a text book with basic linguistic facts about the source language is available (here, Portuguese). We want to test the generality and specificity of the method. Can the systematic commonalities and differences between two genetically related languages be exploited for cross-language applications? Is the processing of Portuguese via Spanish different from the processing of Russian via Czech (Hana et al., 2004; Feldman et al., 2006)?

[1] We thank the anonymous reviewers for their constructive comments on an earlier version of the paper.

	Spanish	Portuguese
1. sg.	canto	canto
2. sg.	cantas	cantas
3. sg.	canta	canta
1. pl.	catamos	cantamos
2. pl.	cantais	cantais
3. pl.	cantan	cantam

Table 1: Verb conjugation present indicative: *-ar* regular verb: *cantar* 'to sing'

2 Brazilian Portuguese (BP) vs. Peninsular Spanish (PS)

Portuguese and Spanish are both Romance languages from the Iberian Peninsula, and share many morpho-syntactic characteristics. Both languages have a similar verb system with three main conjugations (*-ar*, *-er*, *-ir*), nouns and adjectives may vary in number and gender, and adverbs are invariable. Both are pro-drop languages, they have a similar pronominal system, and certain phenomena, such as clitic climbing, are prevalent in both languages. They also allow rather free constituent order; and in both cases there is considerable debate in the literature about the appropriate characterization of their predominant word order (the candidates being SVO and VSO).

Sometimes the languages exhibit near-complete parallelism in their morphological patterns, as shown in Table 1.

The languages are also similar in their lexicon and syntactic word order:

(1) Os estudantes já comparam os livros. [BP]
Los estudiantes ya compraron los libros. [PS]
The students already bought the books
'The students have already bought the books.'

One of the main differences is the fact that Brazilian Portuguese (BP) accepts object dropping, while Peninsular Spanish (PS) doesn't. In addition, subjects in BP tend to be overt while in PS they tend to be omitted.

(2) a. A: O que você fez com o livro? [BP]
What you did with the book?
A: 'What did you do with the book?'
B: *Eu* dei para Maria.
I gave to Mary
B: 'I gave it to Mary.'

b. A: ¿Qué hiciste con el libro? [PS]
What did with the book?
A: 'What did you do with the book?'
B: Se *lo* di a María.
Her.dat it.acc gave to Mary.
B: 'I gave it to Mary.'

Notice also that in the Spanish example (2b) the dative pronoun *se* 'her' is obligatory even when the prepositional phrase *a María* 'to Mary' is present.

3 Resources

3.1 Tagset

For both Spanish and Portuguese, we used positional tagsets developed on the basis of Spanish CLiC-TALP tagset (Torruella, 2002). Every tag is a string of 11 symbols each corresponding to one morphological category. For example, the Portuguese word *partires* 'you leave' is assigned the tag `VM0S---2PI-`, because it is a verb (`V`), main (`M`), gender is not applicable to this verb form (`0`), singular (`S`), case, possesor's number and form are not applicable to this category(`-`), 2nd person (`2`), present (`P`), indicative (`I`) and participle type is not applicable (`-`).

A comparison of the two tagsets is in Table 2.[2] When possible the Spanish and Portuguese tagsets use the same values, however some differences are unavoidable. For instance, the pluperfect is a compound verb tense in Spanish, but a separate word that needs a tag of its own in Portuguese. In addition, we added a tag for "treatment" Portuguese pronouns.

The Spanish tagset has 282 tags, while that for Portuguese has 259 tags.

3.2 Training corpora

Spanish training corpus. The Spanish corpus we use for training the transition probabilities as well as for obtaining Spanish-Portuguese cognate pairs is a fragment (106,124 tokens, 18,629 types) of the Spanish section of CLiC-TALP (Torruella,

[2]Notice that we have 6 possible values for the gender position: `M` (masc.), `F` (fem.), `N` (neutr., for certain pronouns), `C` (common, either `M` or `F`), `0` (unspecified for this form within the category), `-` (the category does not distinguish gender)

No.	Description	No. of values	
		Sp	Po
1	POS	14	11
2	SubPOS – detailed POS	30	29
3	Gender	6	6
4	Number	5	5
5	Case	6	6
6	Possessor's Number	4	4
7	Form	3	3
8	Person	5	5
9	Tense	7	9
10	Mood	8	9
11	Participle	3	3

Table 2: Overview and comparison of the tagsets

2002). CLiC-TALP is a balanced corpus, containing texts of various genres and styles. We automatically translated the CLiC-TALP tagset into our system (see Sect. 3.1) for easier detailed evaluation and for comparison with our previous work that used a similar approach for tagging (Hana et al., 2004; Feldman et al., 2006).

Raw Portuguese corpus. For automatic lexicon acquisition, we use NILC corpus,[3] containing 1.2M tokens.

3.3 Evaluation corpus

For evaluation purposes, we selected and manually annotated a small portion (1,800 tokens) of NILC corpus.

4 Morphological Analysis

Our morphological analyzer (Hana, 2005) is an open and modular system. It allows us to combine modules with different levels of manual input – from a module using a small manually provided lexicon, through a module using a large lexicon automatically acquired from a raw corpus, to a guesser using a list of paradigms, as the only resource provided manually. The general strategy is to run modules that make fewer errors and less overgenerate before modules that make more errors and overgenerate more. This, for example, means that modules with manually created resources are used before modules with resources automatically acquired. In the experiments below, we used the following modules – lookup in a list of (mainly) closed-class words, a paradigm-based guesser and an automatically acquired lexicon.

[3] Núcleo Interdisciplinar de Lingüística Computacional; available at `http://nilc.icmc.sc.usp.br/nilc/`, we used the version with POS tags assigned by PALAVRAS. We ignored the POS tags.

4.1 Portuguese closed class words

We created a list of the most common prepositions, conjunctions, and pronouns, and a number of the most common irregular verbs. The list contains about 460 items and it required about 6 hours of work. In general, the closed class words can be derived either from a reference grammar book, or can be elicited from a native speaker. This does not require native-speaker expertise or intensive linguistic training. The reason why the creation of such a list took 6 hours is that the words were annotated with detailed morphological tags used by our system.

4.2 Portuguese paradigms

We also created a list of morphological paradigms. Our database contains 38 paradigms. We just encoded basic facts about the Portuguese morphology from a standard grammar textbook (Cunha and Cintra, 2001). The paradigms include all three regular verb conjugations (*-ar*, *-er*, *-ir*), the most common adjective and nouns paradigms and a rule for adverbs of manner that end with *-mente* (analogous to the English *-ly*). We ignore majority of exceptions. The creation of the paradigms took about 8 h of work.

4.3 Lexicon Acquisition

The morphological analyzer supports a module or modules employing a lexicon containing information about lemmas, stems and paradigms. There is always the possibility to provide this information manually. That, however, is very costly. Instead, we created such a lexicon automatically.

Usually, automatically acquired lexicons and similar systems are used as a backup for large high-precision high-cost manually created lexicons (e.g. Mikheev, 1997; Hlaváčová, 2001). Such systems extrapolate the information about the words known by the lexicon (e.g. distributional properties of endings) to unknown words. Since our approach is resource light, we do not have any such large lexicon to extrapolate from.

The general idea of our system is very simple. The paradigm-based Guesser, provides all the possible analyses of a word consistent with Portuguese paradigms. Obviously, this approach massively overgenerates. Part of the ambiguity is usually real but most of it is spurious. We use a large corpus to weed the spurious analyses out of the real ones. In such corpus, open-class lemmas are likely to occur in more than one form. Therefore, if a lemma+paradigm candidate suggested by the Guesser occurs in other forms in other parts of the corpus, it increases the likelihood that the candidate is real and vice versa. If we encounter the word *cantamos* 'we sing' in a Portuguese corpus, using the information about the paradigms we can analyze it in two ways, either as being a noun in the plural with the ending *-s*, or as being a verb in the 1st person plural with the ending *-amos*. Based on this single form we cannot say more. However if we also encounter the forms *canto*, *canta*, *cantam* the verb analysis becomes much more probable; and therefore, it will be chosen for the lexicon. If the only forms that we encounter in our Portuguese corpus were *cantamos* and (the non-existing) *cantamo* (such as the existing word *ramo* and *ramos*) then we would analyze it as a noun and not as a verb.

With such an approach, and assuming that the corpus contains the forms of the verb *matar* 'to kill', $mato_{1sg}$ $matas_{2sg}$, $mata_{3sg}$, etc., we would not discover that there is also a noun *mata* 'forest' with a plural form *matas* – the set of the 2 noun forms is a proper subset of the verb forms. A simple solution is to consider not the number of form types covered in a corpus, but the coverage of the possible forms of the particular paradigm. However this brings other problems (e.g. it penalizes paradigms with large number of forms, paradigms with some obsolete forms, etc.). We combine both of these measures in Hana (2005).

Lexicon Acquisition consists of three steps:

1. A large raw corpus is analyzed with a lexicon-less MA (an MA using a list of mainly closed-class words and a paradigm based guesser);

2. All possible hypothetical lexical entries over these analyses are created.

3. Hypothetical entries are filtered with aim to discard as many nonexisting entries as possible, without discarding real entries.

Obviously, morphological analysis based on such a lexicon still overgenerates, but it overgenerates much less than if based on the endings alone.

Lexicon	no	yes
recall	**99.0**	98.1
avg ambig (tag/word)	4.3	**3.5**
Tagging (cognates) – accuracy	79.1	82.1

Table 3: Evaluation of Morphological analysis

Consider for example, the form *funções* 'functions' of the feminine noun *função*. The analyzer without a lexicon provides 11 analyses (6 lemmas, each with 1 to 3 tags); only one of them is correct. In contrast, the analyzer with an automatically acquired lexicon provides only two analyses: the correct one (noun fem. pl.) and an incorrect one (noun masc. pl., note that POS and number are still correct). Of course, not all cases are so persuasive.

The evaluation of the system is in Table 3. The 98.1% recall is equivalent to the upper bound for the task. It is calculated assuming an oracle-Portuguese tagger that is always able to select the correct POS tag if it is in the set of options given by the morphological analyzer. Notice also that for the tagging accuracy, the drop of recall is less important than the drop of ambiguity.

5 Tagging

We used the TnT tagger (Brants, 2000), an implementation of the Viterbi algorithm for second-order Markov model. In the traditional approach, we would train the tagger's transitional and emission probabilities on a large annotated corpus of Portuguese. However, our resource-light approach means that such corpus is not available to us and we need to use different ways to obtain this information.

We assume that syntactic properties of Spanish and Portuguese are similar enough to be able to use the transitional probabilities trained on Spanish (after a simple tagset mapping).

The situation with the lexical properties as captured by emission probabilities is more complex. Below we present three different ways how to obtains emissions, assuming:

1. they are the same: we use the Spanish emissions directly (§5.1).

2. they are different: we ignore the Spanish emissions and instead uniformly distribute

the results of our morphological analyzer. (§5.2)

3. they are similar: we map the Spanish emissions onto the result of morphological analysis using automatically acquired cognates. (§5.3)

5.1 Tagging – Baseline

Our lowerbound measurement consists of training the TnT tagger on the Spanish corpus and applying this model directly to Portuguese.[4] The overall performance of such a tagger is 56.8% (see the the *min* column in Table 4). That means that half of the information needed for tagging of Portuguese is already provided by the Spanish model. This tagger has seen no Portuguese whatsoever, and is still much better than nothing.

5.2 Tagging – Approximating Emissions I

The opposite extreme to the baseline, is to assume that Spanish emissions are useless for tagging Portuguese. Instead we use the morphological analyzer to limit the number of possibilities, treating them all equally – The emission probabilities would then form a uniform distribution of the tags given by the analyzer. The results are summarized in Table 4 (the *e-even* column) – accuracy 77.2% on full tags, or 47% relative error reduction against the baseline.

5.3 Tagging – Approximating Emissions II

Although it is true that forms and distributions of Portuguese and Spanish words are not the same, they are also not completely unrelated. As any Spanish speaker would agree, the knowledge of Spanish words *is* useful when trying to understand a text in Portuguese.

Many of the corresponding Portuguese and Spanish words are cognates, i.e. historically they descend from the same ancestor root or they are mere translations. We assume two things: (i) cognate pairs have usually similar morphological and distributional properties, (ii) cognate words are similar in form.

Obviously both of these assumptions are approximations:

1. Cognates could have departed in their meanings, and thus probably also have different distributions. For example, Spanish *embarazada* 'pregnant' vs. Portuguese *embaraçada* 'embarrassed'.

2. Cognates could have departed in their morphological properties. For example, Spanish *cerca* 'near'.adverb vs. Portuguese *cerca* 'fence'.noun (from Latin *circa*, *circus* 'circle').

3. There are false cognates – unrelated, but similar or even identical words. For example, Spanish *salada* 'salty'.adj vs. Portuguese *salada* 'salad'.noun, Spanish *doce* 'twelve'.numeral vs. Portuguese *doce* 'candy'.noun

Nevertheless, we believe that these examples are true exceptions from the rule and that in majority of cases, the cognates would look and behave similarly. The borrowings, counter-borrowings and parallel developments of the various Romance languages have of course been extensively studied, and we have no space for a detailed discussion.

Identifying cognates. For the present work, however, we do not assume access to philological erudition, or to accurate Spanish-Portuguese translations or even a sentence-aligned corpus. All of these are resources that we could not expect to obtain in a resource poor setting. In the absence of this knowledge, we automatically identify cognates, using the edit distance measure (normalized by word length).

Unlike in the standard edit distance, the cost of operations is dependent on the arguments. Similarly as Yarowsky and Wicentowski (2000), we assume that, in any language, vowels are more mutable in inflection than consonants, thus for example replacing *a* for *i* is cheaper that replacing *s* by *r*. In addition, costs are refined based on some well known and common phonetic-orthographic regularities, e.g. replacing a *q* with *c* is less costly than replacing *m* with, say *s*. However, we do not want to do a detailed contrastive morpho-phonological analysis, since we want our system to be portable to other languages. So, some facts from a simple grammar reference book should be enough.

Using cognates. Having a list of Spanish-Portuguese cognate pairs, we can use these to map the emission probabilities acquired on Spanish corpus to Portuguese.

[4]Before training, we translated the Spanish tagset into the Portuguese one.

Let's assume Spanish word w_s and Portuguese word w_p are cognates. Let T_s denote the tags that w_s occurs within the Spanish corpus, and let $p_s(t)$ be the emission probability of a tag t ($t \notin T_s \Rightarrow p_s(t) = 0$). Let T_p denote tags assigned to the Portuguese word w_p by our morphological analyzer, and the $p_p(t)$ is the even emission probability: $p_p(t) = \frac{1}{|T_p|}$. Then we can assign the new emission probability $p'_p(t)$ to every tag $t \in T_p$ in the following way (followed by normalization):

$$p'_p(t) = \frac{p_s(t) + p_p(t)}{2} \tag{1}$$

Results. This method provides the best results. The full-tag accuracy is 82.1%, compared to 56.9% for baseline (58% error rate reduction) and 77.2% for even-emissions (21% reduction). The accuracy for POS is 87.6%. Detailed results are in column *e-cognates* of Table 4.

	min	e-even	e-cognates
Tag:	56.9	77.2	82.1
POS:	65.3	84.2	87.6
SubPOS:	61.7	83.3	86.9
gender:	70.4	87.3	90.2
number:	78.3	95.3	96.0
case:	93.8	96.8	97.2
possessor's num:	85.4	96.7	97.0
form:	92.9	99.2	99.2
person:	74.5	91.2	92.7
tense:	90.7	95.1	96.1
mood:	91.5	95.0	96.0
participle:	99.9	100.0	100.0

Table 4: Tagging Brazilian Portuguese

6 Evaluation & Comparison

The best way to evaluate our results would be to compare it against the TnT tagger used the usual way – trained on Portuguese and applied on Portuguese. We do not have access to a large Portuguese corpus annotated with detailed tags. However, we believe that Spanish and Portuguese are similar enough (see Sect. 2) to justify our assumption that the TnT tagger would be equally successful (or unsuccessful) on them. The accuracy of TnT trained on 90K tokens of the CLiC-TALP corpus is 94.2% (tested on 16K tokens). The accuracy of our best tagger is 82.1%. Thus the error-rate is more than 3 times bigger (17.9% vs. 5.4%).

Branco and Silva (2003) report 97.2% tagging accuracy on 23K testing corpus. This is clearly better than our results, on the other hand they needed a large Portuguese corpus of 207K tokens. The details of the tagset used in the experiments are not provided, so precise comparison with our results is difficult.

7 Related work

Previous research in resource-light language learning has defined *resource-light* in different ways. Some have assumed only partially tagged training corpora (Merialdo, 1994); some have begun with small tagged seed wordlists (Cucerzan and Yarowsky, 1999) for named-entity tagging, while others have exploited the automatic transfer of an already existing annotated resource in a different genres or a different language (e.g. cross-language projection of morphological and syntactic information in (Yarowsky et al., 2001; Yarowsky and Ngai, 2001), requiring no direct supervision in the target language).

Ngai and Yarowsky (2000) observe that the total weighted human and resource costs is the most practical measure of the degree of supervision. Cucerzan and Yarowsky (2002) observe that another useful measure of minimal supervision is the additional cost of obtaining a desired functionality from existing commonly available knowledge sources. They note that for a remarkably wide range of languages, there exist a plenty of reference grammar books and dictionaries which is an invaluable linguistic resource.

7.1 Resource-light approaches to Romance languages

Cucerzan and Yarowsky (2002) present a method for bootstrapping a fine-grained, broad coverage POS tagger in a new language using only one person-day of data acquisition effort. Similarly to us, they use a basic library reference grammar book, and access to an existing monolingual text corpus in the language, but they also use a medium-sized bilingual dictionary.

In our work, we use a paradigm-based morphology, including only the basic paradigms from a standard grammar textbook. Cucerzan and Yarowsky (2002) create a dictionary of regular inflectional affix changes and their associated POS and on the basis of it, generate hypothesized inflected forms following the regular paradigms.

Clearly, these hypothesized forms are inaccurate and overgenerated. Therefore, the authors perform a probabilistic match from all lexical tokens actually observed in a monolingual corpus and the hypothesized forms. They combine these two models, a model created on the basis of dictionary information and the one produced by the morphological analysis. This approach relies heavily on two assumptions: (i) words of the same POS tend to have similar tag sequence behavior; and (ii) there are sufficient instances of each POS tag labeled by either the morphology models or closed-class entries. For richly inflectional languages, however, there is no guarantee that the latter assumption would always hold.

The accuracy of their model is comparable to ours. On a fine-grained (up to 5-feature) POS space, they achieve 86.5% for Spanish and 75.5% for Romanian. With a tagset of a similar size (11 features) we obtain the accuracy of 82.1% for Portuguese.

Carreras et al. (2003) present work on developing low-cost Named Entity recognizers (NER) for a language with no available annotated resources, using as a starting point existing resources for a similar language. They devise and evaluate several strategies to build a Catalan NER system using only annotated Spanish data and unlabeled Catalan text, and compare their approach with a classical bootstrapping setting where a small initial corpus in the target language is hand tagged. It turns out that the hand translation of a Spanish model is better than a model directly learned from a small hand annotated training corpus of Catalan. The best result is achieved using cross-linguistic features. Solorio and López (2005) follow their approach; however, they apply the NER system for Spanish directly to Portuguese and train a classifier using the output and the real classes.

7.2 Cognates

Mann and Yarowsky (2001) present a method for inducing translation lexicons based on trasduction modules of cognate pairs via bridge languages. Bilingual lexicons within language families are induced using probabilistic string edit distance models. Translation lexicons for abitrary distant language pairs are then generated by a combination of these intra-family translation models and one or more cross-family online dictionaries. Similarly to Mann and Yarowsky (2001), we show that languages are often close enough to others within their language family so that cognate pairs between the two are common, and significant portions of the translation lexicon can be induced with high accuracy where no bilingual dictionary or parallel corpora may exist.

8 Conclusion

We have shown that a tagging system with a small amount of manually created resources can be successful. We have previously shown that this approach can work for Czech and Russian (Hana et al., 2004; Feldman et al., 2006). Here we have shown its applicability to a new language pair. This can be done in a fraction of the time needed for systems with extensive manually created resources: days instead of years. Three resources are required: (i) a reference grammar (for information about paradigms and closed class words); (ii) a large amount of text (for learning a lexicon; e.g. newspapers from the internet); (iii) a limited access to a native speaker — reference grammars are often too vague and a quick glance at results can provide feedback leading to a significant increase of accuracy; however both of these require only limited linguistic knowledge.

In this paper we proposed an algorithm for cognate transfer that effectively projects the source language emission probabilities into the target language. Our experiments use minimal new human effort and show 21% error reduction over even emissions on a fine-grained tagset.

In the near future, we plan to compare the effectiveness (time and price) of our approach with that of the standard resource-intensive approach to annotating a medium-size corpus (on a corpus of around 100K tokens). A resource-intensive system will be more accurate in the labels which it offers to the annotator, so annotator can work faster (there are fewer choices to make, fewer keystrokes required). On the other hand, creation of the infrastructure for such a system is very time consuming and may not be justified by the intended application.

The experiments that we are running right now are supposed to answer the question of whether training the system on a small corpus of a closely related language is better than training on a larger corpus of a less related language. Some preliminary results (Feldman et al., 2006) suggest that using cross-linguistic features leads to higher precision, especially for the source languages which have target-like properties complementary to each other.

9 Acknowledgments

We would like to thank Maria das Graças Volpe Nunes, Sandra Maria Aluísio, and Ricardo Hasegawa for giving us access to the NILC corpus annotated with PALAVRAS and to Carlos Rodríguez Penagos for letting us use the Spanish part of the CLiC-TALP corpus.

References

Branco, A. and J. Silva (2003). Portuguese-specific Issues in the Rapid Development of State-of-the-art Taggers. In *Workshop on Tagging and Shallow Processing of Portuguese: TASHA'2000.*

Brants, T. (2000). TnT – A Statistical Part-of-Speech Tagger. In *Proceedings of ANLP-NAACL*, pp. 224–231.

Carreras, X., L. Màrquez, and L. Padró (2003). Named Entity Recognition for Catalan Using Only Spanish Resources and Unlabelled Data. In *Proceedings of EACL-2003.*

Cucerzan, S. and D. Yarowsky (1999). Language Independent Named Entity Recognition Combining Morphological and Contextual Evidence. In *Proceedings of the 1999 Joint SIGDAT Conference on EMNLP and VLC*, pp. 90–99.

Cucerzan, S. and D. Yarowsky (2002). Bootstrapping a Multilingual Part-of-speech Tagger in One Person-day. In *Proceedings of CoNLL 2002*, pp. 132–138.

Cunha, C. and L. F. L. Cintra (2001). *Nova Gramática do Português Contemporâneo.* Rio de Janeiro, Brazil: Nova Fronteira.

Feldman, A., J. Hana, and C. Brew (2006). Experiments in Morphological Annotation Transfer. In *Proceedings of Computational Linguistics and Intelligent Text Processing (CICLing).*

Hana, J. (2005). Knowledge and labor light morphological analysis. Unpublished manuscript.

Hana, J., A. Feldman, and C. Brew (2004). A Resource-light Approach to Russian Morphology: Tagging Russian using Czech resources. In *Proceedings of EMNLP 2004*, Barcelona, Spain.

Hlaváčová, J. (2001). Morphological Guesser or Czech Words. In V. Matoušek (Ed.), *Text, Speech and Dialogue*, Lecture Notes in Computer Science, pp. 70–75. Berlin: Springer-Verlag.

Hwa, R., P. Resnik, A. Weinberg, C. Cabezas, and O. Kolak (2004). Bootstrapping Parsers via Syntactic Projection across Parallel Texts. *Natural Language Engineering 1*(1), 1–15.

Mann, G. S. and D. Yarowsky (2001). Multipath Translation Lexicon via Bridge Languages. In *Proceedings of NAACL 2001.*

Merialdo, B. (1994). Tagging English Text with a Probabilistic Model. *Computational Linguistics 20*(2), 155–172.

Meurers, D. (2004). On the Use of Electronic Corpora for Theoretical Linguistics. Case Studies from the Syntax of German. *Lingua.*

Mikheev, A. (1997). Automatic Rule Induction for Unknown Word Guessing. *Computational Linguistics 23*(3), 405–423.

Ngai, G. and D. Yarowsky (2000). Rule Writing or Annotation: Cost-efficient Resource Usage for Base Noun Phrase Chunking. In *Proceedings of the 38th Meeting of ACL*, pp. 117–125.

Solorio, T. and A. L. López (2005). Learning named entity recognition in Portuguese from Spanish. In *Proceedings of Computational Linguistics and Intelligent Text Processing (CICLing).*

Torruella, M. (2002). Guía para la anotación morfológica del corpus CLiC-TALP (Versión 3). Technical Report WP-00/06, X-Tract Working Paper.

Yarowsky, D. and G. Ngai (2001). Inducing Multilingual POS Taggers and NP Bracketers via Robust Projection Across Aligned Corpora. In *Proceedings of NAACL-2001*, pp. 200–207.

Yarowsky, D., G. Ngai, and R. Wicentowski (2001). Inducing Multilingual Text Analysis Tools via Robust Projection across Aligned Corpora. In *Proceedings of HLT 2001, First International Conference on Human Language Technology Research.*

Yarowsky, D. and R. Wicentowski (2000). Minimally supervised morphological analysis by multimodal alignment. In *Proceedings of the 38th Meeting of the Association for Computational Linguistics*, pp. 207–216.

Automatic Generation of Translation Dictionaries Using Intermediary Languages

Kisuh Ahn and Matthew Frampton
ICCS, School of Informatics
Edinburgh University
K.Ahn@sms.ed.ac.uk,M.J.E.Frampton@sms.ed.ac.uk

Abstract

We describe a method which uses one or more intermediary languages in order to automatically generate translation dictionaries. Such a method could potentially be used to efficiently create translation dictionaries for language groups which have as yet had little interaction. For any given word in the source language, our method involves first translating into the intermediary language(s), then into the target language, back into the intermediary language(s) and finally back into the source language. The relationship between a word and the number of possible translations in another language is most often 1-to-many, and so at each stage, the number of possible translations grows exponentially. If we arrive back at the same starting point i.e. the same word in the source language, then we hypothesise that the meanings of the words in the chain have not diverged significantly. Hence we backtrack through the link structure to the target language word and accept this as a suitable translation. We have tested our method by using English as an intermediary language to automatically generate a Spanish-to-German dictionary, and the results are encouraging.

1 Introduction

In this paper we describe a method which uses one or more intermediary languages to automatically generate a dictionary to translate from one language, X, to another, Y. The method relies on using dictionaries that can connect X to Y and back to X via the intermediary language(s), e.g. $X \rightarrow IL$, $IL \rightarrow Y$, $Y \rightarrow IL$, $IL \rightarrow X$, where IL is an intermediary language such as English. The resources required to exploit the method are not difficult to find since dictionaries already exist that translate between English and a vast number of other languages. Whereas at present the production of translation dictionaries is manual (e.g. (Serasset1994)), our method is automatic. We believe that projects such as (Boitet *et al.*2002) and (Wiktionary), which are currently generating translation dictionaries by hand could benefit greatly from using our method. Translation dictionaries are useful not only for end-user consumption but also for various multilingual tasks such as cross-language question answering (e.g. (Ahn *et al.*2004)) and information retrieval (e.g. (Argaw *et al.*2004)). We have applied our method to automatically generate a Spanish-to-German dictionary. We chose this language pair because we were able to find an online Spanish-to-German dictionary which could be used to evaluate our result.

The structure of the paper is as follows. In section 2.1, we describe how if we translate a word from a source language into an intermediary language, and then into a target language, the number of possible translations may grow drastically. Some of these translations will be 'better' than others, and in section 2.2 we give a detailed description of our method for identifying these 'better' translations. Having identified the 'better' translations we can then automatically generate a dictionary that translates directly from the source to the target language. In section 3 we describe how we used our method to automatically generate a Spanish-to-German dictionary, and in section 3.3, we evaluate the result. Finally, in section 4, we conclude and suggest future work.

2 Translating Via An Intermediary Language

2.1 The Problem

Consider the problem of finding the different possible translations for a word x from language X in language Y when there is no available $X \rightarrow Y$ dictionary. Let us assume that there are dictionaries which allow us to connect from X to Y and back to X via an intermediary language IL i.e. dictionaries for $X \rightarrow IL$, $IL \rightarrow Y$, $Y \rightarrow IL$ and $IL \rightarrow X$, as shown in figure 1.

If there was only ever 1 suitable translation for any given word in another language, then it would be trivial to use dictionaries $X \rightarrow IL$ and $IL \rightarrow Y$ in order to obtain a translation of x in language Y. However, this is not the case - for any given word x in language X the $X \rightarrow IL$ dictionary will usually give multiple possible translations $(il_1 ... il_n)$, some of which diverge more than others in meaning from x. The $IL \rightarrow Y$ dictionary will then produce multiple possible translations for each of $(il_1 ... il_n)$ to give $(y_1 ... y_p)$ where $p >= n$. Again, some of $(y_1 ... y_p)$ will diverge more than oth-

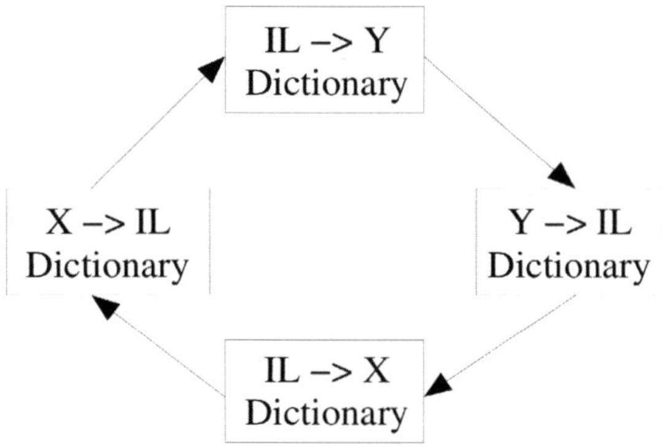

Figure 1: The cycle of dictionaries

ers in meaning from their source words in $(il_1...il_n)$. Hence we have p possible translations of the word x from language X in language Y. Some of $(y_1...y_p)$ will have diverged less in meaning than others from x, and so can be considered 'better' translations. The problem then is how to identify these 'better' translations.

2.2 Using The Link Structure To Find 'Better' Translations

Our method for identifying the 'better' translations is to first use dictionary $Y \rightarrow IL$ to produce $(il2_1...il2_q)$, the multiple possible translations of each of $(y_1...y_m)$, where $q >= m$. Next we use dictionary $IL \rightarrow X$ to give $(x2_1...x2_r)$, the multiple translations of each of $(il2_1...il2_q)$, where $r >= q$. We then select each of the members of the set $(x2_1...x2_r)$ which are equal to the original word x. We hypothesise that to have returned to the same starting word, the meanings of the words that have formed a chain through the link structure cannot have diverged significantly, and so we retrace two steps to the word in $(y_1...y_m)$ and accept this as a suitable translation of x. Figure 2 represents a hypothetical case in which two members of the set $(x2_1...x2_r)$ are equal to the original word x. We retrace our route from these through the links to y_1 and y_2, and we accept these as suitable translations.

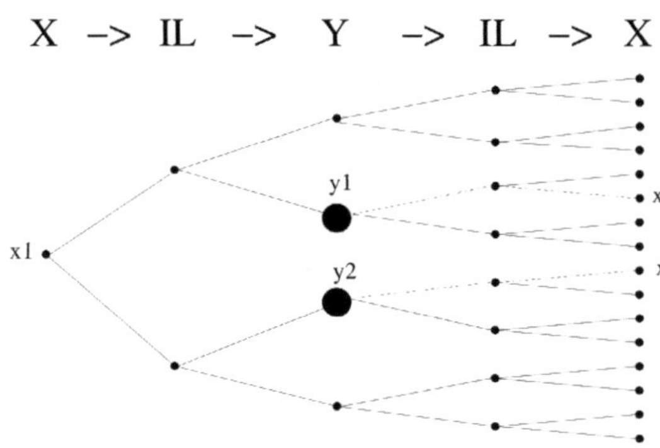

Figure 2: Translating from $X \rightarrow IL \rightarrow Y \rightarrow IL \rightarrow X$. Nodes are possible translations.

If we apply the method described here to a large number of words from language X then we can automatically generate a language X-to-language Y dictionary. Here we have considered using just one intermediary language, but provided we have the dictionaries to complete a cycle from X to Y and back to X, then we can use any number of intermediary languages, e.g. $X \rightarrow IL$, $IL \rightarrow IL2$, $IL2 \rightarrow IL$, $IL \rightarrow Y$, where $IL2$ is a second intermediary language.

3 The Experiment

We have applied the method described in section 2 in order to automatically generate a Spanish-to-German dictionary using Spanish-to-English, English-to-German, German-to-English and English-to-Spanish dictionaries. We chose Spanish and German because we were able to find an online Spanish-to-German dictionary which could be used to evaluate our automatically-generated dictionary.

3.1 Obtaining The Data

We first collected large lists of German and English lemmas from the Celex Database, ((Baayen and Gulikers1995)). We also gathered a short list of Spanish lemmas, all starting with the letter 'a' from the Wiktionary website (Wiktionary) to use as our starting terms. We created our own dictionaries by making use of online dictionaries. In order to obtain the English translations for the German lemmas and vice versa, we queried 'The New English-German Dictionary' site of The Technical Universiy of Dresden [1]. To obtain the English translations for the Spanish lemmas and vice versa, we queried 'The Spanish Dict' website [2]. Finally, we wanted to compare the performance of our automatically-generated Spanish-to-German dictionary with that of a manually-generated Spanish-to-German dictionary, and for this we used a website called 'DIX: Deutsch-Spanisch Woerterbuch' [3]. Table 1 gives information about the four dictionaries which we created in order to automatically generate our Spanish-to-German dictionary. The fifth is the manually-generated dictionary used for evaluation.

Dicts	Ents	Trans	Trans/term
S to E	664	1202	1.8
E to S	18845	28300	1.5
G to E	27918	77626	2.8
E to G	26298	104693	4.0
S to G'	610	3126	5.1

Table 1: Dictionaries; S = Spanish, E = English, G = German, S to G' is the dictionary used for evaluation.

[1] http://www.iee.et.tu-dresden.de/cgi-bin/cgiwrap/wernerr/search.sh

[2] http://www.spanishdict.com/

[3] http://dix.osola.com/

3.2 Automatically Generating The Dictionary

For our experiment, we used the method described in section 2 to automatically construct a scaled-down version of a Spanish-to-German dictionary. It contained 664 Spanish terms, all starting with the letter 'a'. To store and operate on the data, we used the open source database program PostgresSQL, version 7.3.4. Starting with the Spanish-to-English dictionary, at each of stages $1-3$, we produced a new dictionary table with an additional column to the right for the new language. We did this by using the appropriate dictionary to look up the translations for the terms in the old rightmost column, before inserting these translations into a new rightmost column. For example, to create the Spanish-to-English-to-German (SEG) table, we used the English-to-German dictionary to find the translations for the English terms in the Spanish-to-English (SE) table, and then inserted these translations into a new rightmost column. We kept producing new tables in this fashion until we had generated a Spanish-to-English-to-German-to-English-to-Spanish (SEGES) table. In stage 4, the final stage, we selected only those rows in which the starting and ending Spanish terms were the same. Important characteristics of these dictionary tables are given in table 2.

Stages	Dicts	Ents	Trans	Trans/term
0	SE	664	1202	1.8
1	SEG	631	6966	11.0
2	SEGE	568	24012	42.3
3	SEGES	566	38002	67.1
4	SEGES	533	4313	8.1

Table 2: Constructing Dictionary; Ents = number of entries, Trans = number of translations, Trans/term = average number of translations given per entry.

Table 2 shows that the number of translations-per-term grew and grew from 1.8 translations in the starting Spanish-to-English dictionary to an enormous 67.1 translations per term in the SEGES table after stage 3. However, after stage 4, having selected only those rows with matching first and last entries for Spanish, we reduced the number of translations back to 8.1 per term.

3.3 Evaluation

Having automatically generated the Spanish-to-German dictionary containing 533 unique Spanish terms, we then compared it to the manually-generated Spanish-to-German dictionary (see section 3.1). We gave the same initial 664 Spanish terms to the manually-generated dictionary but received translations for only 610.

The results are summarised in table 3. We observe that when we regard the manually-generated dictionary as the Gold-standard, our automatically-generated dictionary managed to produce a relatively adequate coverage of some 73.6% (392 out of 533) with respect to main entries overlap between the two dictionaries. When we look at the number of translations per term, we find that our dictionary covered most of the translations found in the manually-generated dictionary (4.0 out of 5.1 average or 78.4%) for which there was a corresponding entry in our dictionary. In fact, our dictionary produced more translations-per-term than the manually-generated one. An extra translation may be an error or it may not appear in the manually-generated dictionary because the manually-generated dictionary is too sparse. Further evaluation is required in order to assess how many of the extra translations were errors.

	Auto SG	Man SG	Overlap
Entries	533	610	392 (73.6%)
Total Trans	4313	3126	1577
Trans/Entry	8.1	5.1	4.0 (78.4%)

Table 3: Result: SG automatic vs SG manual

In conclusion, we find that our automatically-generated dictionary has an adequate but not perfect coverage and very good recall for each term covered within our dictionary. As for the precision of the translations found, we need more investigation and perhaps a more complete manually-generated comparison dictionary. The results might have been even better had it not been for several problems with the four starting dictionaries. For example, a translation for a particular word could sometimes not be found as an entry in the next dictionary. This might be because the entry simply wasn't present, or because of different conventions e.g. listing verbs as "to Z" when another simply gives "Z". Another cause was differences in font encoding e.g. with German umlauts. Results might also have improved had the starting dictionaries provided more translations per entry term, and had we used part-of-speech information - this was impossible since not all of the dictionaries listed part-of-speech. All in all given the fact that the quality of data with which we started was far from ideal, we believe that our method shows great promise for saving human labour in the construction of translation dictionaries.

4 Conclusion

In this paper we have described a method using one or more intermediary languages to automatically generate a dictionary to translate from one language, X, to another, Y. The method relies on using dictionaries that can connect X to Y and back to X via the intermediary language(s). We applied the method to automatically generate a Spanish-to-German dictionary, and desptite the limitations of our starting dictionaries, the result seems to be reasonably good. As was stated in section 3.3, we did not evaluate whether translations we generated that were not in the gold-standard manual dictionary were errors or good translations. This is essential future work. We also intend to empirically test what happens when further intermediary dictionaries are introduced into the chain.

We believe that our method can make a great contribution to the construction of translation dictionaries. Even if a dictionary produced by our method is not considered quite complete or accurate enough for general use, it can serve as a very good starting point, thereby saving a great deal of human labour - human labour that requires a large amount of linguistic expertise. Our method could be used to produce translation dictionaries for relatively unconnected language groups, most likely by using English as an intermediary language. Such translation dictionaries could be important in promoting communication between these language groups and an ever more globalised and interconnected world.

A final point to make regards applying our method more generally outside of the domain of translation dictionary construction. We believe that our method, which makes use of link structures, could be applied in different areas involving graphs.

References

Kisuh Ahn, Beatrix Alex, Johan Bos, Tiphaine Dalmas, Jochen L. Leidner, Matthew B. Smillie, and Bonnie Webber. Cross-lingual question answering with qed. 2004.

Atelach Alemu Argaw, Lars Asker, Richard Coester, and Jussi Kalgren. Dictionary based amharic - english information retrieval. 2004.

R.H. Baayen and L. Gulikers. The celex lexical database (release 2). In *Distriubted by the Linguistic Data Consortium*, 1995.

Christian Boitet, Mathieu Mangeot, and Gilles Serasset. The papillon project: Cooperatively building a multilingual lexical data-base to derive open source dictionaries and lexicons. In *2nd Workshop NLPXML*, pages 93–96, Taipei, Taiwan, September 2002.

Gilles Serasset. Interlingual lexical organization for multilingual lexical databases. In *Proceedings of 15th International Conference on Computational Linguistics, COLING-94*, pages 5–9, Aug 1994.

Wiktionary. A wiki based open content dictionary. In *http://www.wiktionary.org/.*

Word Sense Disambiguation Using Automatically Translated Sense Examples

Xinglong Wang
School of Informatics
University of Edinburgh
2 Buccleuch Place, Edinburgh
EH8 9LW, UK
xwang@inf.ed.ac.uk

David Martinez
Department of Computer Science
University of Sheffield
Sheffield, S1 4DP, UK
davidm@dcs.shef.ac.uk

Abstract

We present an unsupervised approach to Word Sense Disambiguation (WSD). We automatically acquire English sense examples using an English-Chinese bilingual dictionary, Chinese monolingual corpora and Chinese-English machine translation software. We then train machine learning classifiers on these sense examples and test them on two gold standard English WSD datasets, one for binary and the other for fine-grained sense identification. On binary disambiguation, performance of our unsupervised system has approached that of the state-of-the-art supervised ones. On multi-way disambiguation, it has achieved a very good result that is competitive to other state-of-the-art unsupervised systems. Given the fact that our approach does not rely on manually annotated resources, such as sense-tagged data or parallel corpora, the results are very promising.

1 Introduction

Results from recent Senseval workshops have shown that supervised Word Sense Disambiguation (WSD) systems tend to outperform their unsupervised counterparts. However, supervised systems rely on large amounts of accurately sense-annotated data to yield good results and such resources are very costly to produce. It is difficult for supervised WSD systems to perform well and reliably on words that do not have enough sense-tagged training data. This is the so-called knowledge acquisition bottleneck.

To overcome this bottleneck, unsupervised WSD approaches have been proposed. Among them, systems under the multilingual paradigm have shown great promise (Gale et al., 1992; Dagan and Itai, 1994; Diab and Resnik, 2002; Ng et al., 2003; Li and Li, 2004; Chan and Ng, 2005; Wang and Carroll, 2005). The underlying hypothesis is that mappings between word forms and meanings can be different from language to language. Much work have been done on extracting sense examples from parallel corpora for WSD. For example, Ng et al. (2003) proposed to train a classifier on sense examples acquired from word-aligned English-Chinese parallel corpora. They grouped senses that share the same Chinese translation, and then the occurrences of the word on the English side of the parallel corpora were considered to have been disambiguated and "sense tagged" by the appropriate Chinese translations. Their system was evaluated on the nouns in Senseval-2 English lexical sample dataset, with promising results. Their follow-up work (Chan and Ng, 2005) has successfully scaled up the approach and achieved very good performance on the Senseval-2 English all-word task.

Despite the promising results, there are problems with relying on parallel corpora. For example, there is a lack of matching occurrences for some Chinese translations to English senses. Thus gathering training examples for them might be difficult, as reported in (Chan and Ng, 2005). Also, parallel corpora themselves are rare resources and not available for many language pairs.

Some researchers seek approaches using monolingual resources in a second language and then try to map the two languages using bilingual dictionaries. For example, Dagan and Itai (1994) carried out WSD experiments using monolingual corpora, a bilingual lexicon and a parser for the source language. One problem of this method is that for many languages, accurate parsers do not exist. Wang and Carroll (2005) proposed to use monolingual corpora and bilingual dictionaries to automatically acquire sense examples. Their system was unsupervised and achieved very promising results on the Senseval-2 lexical sample dataset. Their system also has better portability, i.e., it runs on any language pair as long as a bilingual dictionary is available. However, sense examples acquired using the dictionary-based word-by-word translation can only provide "bag-of-words" features. Many other features useful for machine learning (ML) algorithms, such as the ordering of words, part-of-speech (POS), bigrams, etc., have been lost. It could be more interesting to translate Chinese text snippets using machine translation (MT) software, which would provide richer contextual information that might be useful for WSD learners. Although MT systems themselves are expensive to build, once they are available, they can be used repeatedly to automatically generate as much data as we want. This is an advantage over relying on other expensive resources such as manually sense-tagged data and parallel copora, which are limited in size and producing additional data normally involves further costly investments.

We carried out experiments on acquiring sense examples using both MT software and a bilingual dictionary. When we had the two sets of sense examples ready, we trained a ML classifier on them and then tested them on coarse-grained and fine-grained gold standard WSD datasets, respectively. We found that on both test datasets the classifier using MT translated sense examples outperformed the one using those translated by a dictionary, given the same amount of training examples used on each word sense. This confirms our assumption that a richer feature set, although from a noisy data source, such as machine translated text, might help ML algorithms. In addition, both systems performed very well comparing to other state-of-the-art WSD systems. As we expected, our system is particularly good on coarse-grained disambiguation. Being an unsupervised approach, it achieved a performance competitive to state-of-the-art supervised systems.

This paper is organised as follows: Section 2 revisits the process of acquiring sense examples proposed in (Wang and Carroll, 2005) and then describes our adapted approach. Section 3 outlines resources, the ML algorithm and evaluation metrics that we used. Section 4 and Section 5 detail experiments we carried out on gold standard datasets. We also report our results and error analysis. Finally, Section 6 concludes the paper and draws future directions.

2 Acquisition of Sense Examples

Wang and Carroll (2005) proposed an automatic approach to acquire sense examples from large amount of Chinese text and English-Chinese and Chinese-English dictionaries. The acquisition process is summarised as follows:

1. Translate an English ambiguous word w to Chinese, using an English-Chinese lexicon. Given the assumption that mappings between words and senses are different between English and Chinese, each sense s_i of w maps to a distinct Chinese word. At the end of this step, we have produced a set C, which consists of Chinese words $\{c_1, c_2, ..., c_n\}$, where c_i is the translation corresponding to sense s_i of w, and n is the number of senses that w has.
2. Query large Chinese corpora or/and a search engine using each element in C. For each c_i in C, we collect the text snippets retrieved and construct a Chinese corpus.
3. Word-segment these Chinese text snippets.
4. Use an electronic Chinese-English lexicon to translate the Chinese corpora constructed word by word to English.

This process can be completely automatic and unsupervised. However, in order to compare the performance against other WSD systems, one needs to map senses in the bilingual dictionary to those used by gold standard datasets, which are often from WordNet (Fellbaum, 1998). This step is inevitable unless we use senses in the bilingual dictionary as gold standard. Fortunately, the mapping process only takes a very short time[1], comparing to the effort that it would take to manually sense annotate training examples. At the end of the acquisition process, for each sense s_i of an ambiguous word w, we have a large set of English contexts. Note that a context is represented by a bag of words only. We mimicked this process and built a set of sense examples.

To obtain a richer set of features, we adapted the above process and carried out another acquisition experiment. When translating Chinese text snippets to English in the 4th step, we used MT software instead of a bilingual dictionary. The intuition is that although machine translated text contains noise, features like word ordering, POS tags

[1]A similar process took 15 minutes per noun as reported in (Chan and Ng, 2005), and about an hour for 20 nouns as reported in (Wang and Carroll, 2005).

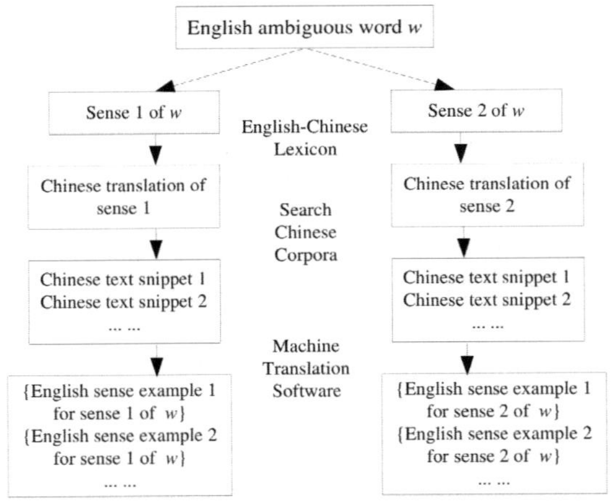

Figure 1:Adapted process of automatic acquisition of sense examples. For simplicity, assume w has two senses.

and bigrams/trigrams may still be of some use for ML classifiers. In this approach, the 3rd step can be omitted, since MT software should be able to take care of segmentation. Figure 1 illustrates our adapted acquisition process.

As described above, we prepared two sets of training examples for each English word sense to disambiguate: one set was translated word-by-word by looking up a bilingual dictionary, as proposed in (Wang and Carroll, 2005), and the other translated using MT software. In detail, we first mapped senses of ambiguous words, as defined in the gold-standard TWA (Mihalcea, 2003) and Senseval-3 lexical sample (Mihalcea et al., 2004) datasets (which we use for evaluation) onto their corresponding Chinese translations. We did this by looking up an English-Chinese dictionary *PowerWord 2002*[2]. This mapping process involved human intervention, but it only took an annotator (fluent speaker in both Chinese and English) 4 hours. Since some Chinese translations are also ambiguous, which may affect WSD performance, the annotator was asked to select the Chinese words that are relatively unambiguous (or ideally monosemous) in Chinese for the target word senses, when it was possible. Sometimes multiple senses of an English word can map to the same Chinese word, according to the English-Chinese dictionary. In such cases, the annotator was advised to try to capture the subtle difference between these English word senses and then to select different Chinese translations for them, using his knowledge on the languages. Then, using the translations as queries, we retrieved as many text snippets as possible from *the Chinese Gigaword Corpus*. For efficiency purposes, we randomly chose maximumly 200 text snippets for each sense, when acquiring data for nouns and adjectives from Senseval-3 lexical sample dataset. The length of the snippets was set to 400 Chinese characters.

From here we prepared two sets of sense examples differently. For the approach of dictionary-based translation, we segmented all text snippets, using the application *ICTCLAS*[3]. After the segmentor marked all word boundaries, the system automatically translated the text snippets word by word using the electronic *LDC Mandarin-English Translation Lexicon 3.0*. All possible translations of each word were included. As expected, the lexicon does not cover all Chinese words. We simply discarded those Chinese words that do not have an entry in this lexicon. We also discarded those Chinese words with multiword English translations. Finally we got a set of sense examples for each sense. Note that a sense example produced here is simply a bag of words without ordering.

We prepared the other set of sense examples by translating text snippets with the MT software *Systran* 5.0 *Standard*, where each example contains much richer features that potentially can be exploited by ML algorithms.

3 Experimental Settings

3.1 Training

We applied the Vector Space Model (VSM) algorithm on the two different kinds of sense examples (i.e., dictionary translated ones vs. MT software translated ones), as it has been shown to perform well with the features described below (Agirre and Martinez, 2004a). In VSM, we represent each context as a vector, where each feature has an 1 or 0 value to indicate its occurrence or absence. For each sense in training, a centroid vector is obtained, and these centroids are compared to the vectors that represent test examples, by means of the cosine similarity function. The closest centroid assigns its sense to the test example.

For the sense examples translated by MT software, we analysed the sentences using different

[2]PowerWord is a commercial electronic dictionary application. There is a free online version at: http://cb.kingsoft.com.

[3]See: http://mtgroup.ict.ac.cn/~zhp/ICTCLAS

tools and extracted relevant features. We applied stemming and POS tagging, using the fnTBL toolkit (Ngai and Florian, 2001), as well as shallow parsing[4]. Then we extracted the following types of topical and domain features[5], which were then fed to the VSM machine learner:

- Topical features: we extracted lemmas of the content words in two windows around the target word: the whole context and a ± 4 word window. We also obtained salient bigrams in the context, with the methods and the software described in (Pedersen, 2001). We included another feature type, which match the closest words (for each POS and in both directions) to the target word (e.g. *LEFT NOUN "dog"* or *LEFT VERB "eat"*).
- Domain features: The "WordNet Domains" resource was used to identify the most relevant domains in the context. Following the relevance formula presented in (Magnini and Cavagliá, 2000), we defined two feature types: (1) the most relevant domain, and (2) a list of domains above a threshold[6].

For the dictionary-translated sense examples, we simply used bags of words as features.

3.2 Evaluation

We evaluated our WSD classifier on both coarse-grained and fine-grained datasets. For coarse-grained WSD evaluation, we used TWA dataset (Mihalcea, 2003), which is a binarily sense-tagged corpus drawn from the British National Corpus (BNC), for 6 nouns. For fine-grained evaluation, we used Senseval-3 English lexical sample dataset (Mihalcea et al., 2004), which comprises 7,860 sense-tagged instances for training and 3,944 for testing, on 57 words (nouns, verbs and adjectives). The examples were mainly drawn from BNC. WordNet 1.7.1[7] was used as sense inventory for nouns and adjectives, and *Wordsmyth*[8] for verbs. We only evaluated our WSD systems on nouns and adjectives.

We also used the SemCor corpus (Miller et al., 1993) for tuning our relative-threshold heuristic. It contains a number of texts, mainly from the Brown Corpus, comprising about 200,000 words, where all content words have been manually tagged with senses from WordNet.

Throughout the paper we will use the concepts of precision and recall to measure the performance of WSD systems, where precision refers to the ratio of correct answers to the total number of answers given by the system, and recall indicates the ratio of correct answers to the total number of instances. Our ML systems attempt every instance and always give a unique answer, and hence precision equals to recall. When comparing with other systems that participated in Senseval-3 in Table 7, both recall and precision are shown. When POS and overall averages are given, they are calculated by micro-averaging the number of examples per word.

4 Experiments on TWA dataset

First we trained a VSM classifier on the sense examples translated with the *Systran* MT software (we use notion "MT-based approach" to refer to this process), and then tested it on the TWA test dataset. We tried two combinations of features: one only used topical features and the other used the whole feature set (i.e., topical and domain features). Table 1 summarises the sizes of the training/test data, the Most Frequent Sense (MFS) baseline and performances when applying the two different feature combinations. We can see that best results were obtained when using all the features. It also shows that both our systems achieved a significant improvement over the MFS baseline. Therefore, in the subsequent WSD experiments following the MT-based approach, we decided to use the entire feature set. To compare the machine-translated sense examples with the ones translated word-by-word, we then trained the same VSM classifier on the examples translated with a bilingual dictionary (we use notion "dictionary-based approach" to refer to this process) and evaluated it on the same test dataset. Table 2 shows results of the dictionary-based approach and the MT-based approach. For comparison, we include results from another system (Mihalcea, 2003), which uses monosemous relatives to automatically acquire sense examples. The right-most column shows results of a 10-fold

[4]This software was kindly provided by David Yarowsky's group at Johns Hopkins University.

[5]Preliminary experiments using local features (bigrams and trigrams) showed low performance, which was expected because of noise in the automatically acquired data.

[6]This software was kindly provided by Gerard Escudero's group at Universitat Politecnica de Catalunya. The threshold was set in previous work.

[7]http://wordnet.princeton.edu

[8]http://www.wordsmyth.net

Word	Train ex.	Test ex.	MFS	Topical	All
bass	3,201	107	90.7	92.5	93.5
crane	3,656	95	74.7	84.2	83.2
motion	2,821	201	70.1	78.6	84.6
palm	1,220	201	71.1	82.6	85.1
plant	4,183	188	54.4	76.6	76.6
tank	3,898	201	62.7	79.1	77.1
Overall	18,979	993	70.6	81.1	82.5

Table 1:Recall(%) of the VSM classifier trained on the MT-translated sense examples, with different sets of features. The MFS baseline(%) and the number of training and test examples are also shown.

Word	(Mihalcea, 2003)	Dictionary-based	MT-based	Hand-tagged
bass	92.5	91.6	93.5	90.7
crane	71.6	74.5	83.2	81.1
motion	75.6	72.6	84.6	93.0
palm	80.6	81.1	85.1	87.6
plant	69.1	51.6	76.6	87.2
tank	63.7	66.7	77.1	84.1
Overall	76.6	71.3	82.5	87.6

Table 2:Recall(%) on TWA dataset for 3 unsupervised systems and a supervised cross-validation on test data.

cross-validation on the TWA data, which indicates the score that a supervised system would attain, taking additional advantage that the examples for training and test are drawn from the same corpus.

We can see that our MT-based approach has achieved significantly better recall than the other two automatic methods. Besides, the results of our unsupervised system are approaching the performance achieved with hand-tagged data. It is worth mentioning that Mihalcea (2003) applied a similar supervised cross-validation method on this dataset that scored 83.35%, very close to our unsupervised system[9]. Thus, we can conclude that the MT-based system is able to reach the best performance reported on this dataset for an unsupervised system.

5 Experiments on Senseval-3

In this section we describe the experiments carried out on the Senseval-3 lexical sample dataset. First, we introduce a heuristic method to deal with the problem of fine-grainedness of WordNet senses. The remaining two subsections will be devoted to the experiments of the baseline system and the contribution of the heuristic to the final system.

[9]The main difference to our hand-tagged evaluation, apart from the ML algorithm, is that we did not remove the bias from the "one sense per discourse" factor, as she did.

Threshold	Remove Senses	Remove Tokens	Sn.-Tk. ratio
4	7,669 (40.6)	11,154 (15.9)	2.55
5	9,759 (51.6)	15,516 (22.1)	2.34
6	11,341 (60.0)	18,827 (26.8)	2.24
7	12,569 (66.5)	21,775 (31.0)	2.14
8	13,553 (71.7)	24,224 (34.5)	2.08
9	14,376 (76.0)	27,332 (38.9)	1.95
10	14,914 (78.9)	29,418 (41.9)	1.88

Table 3:Sense filtering by relative-threshold on SemCor. For each threshold the number of removed senses/tokens and ambiguity are shown.

5.1 Unsupervised methods on fine-grained senses

When applying unsupervised WSD algorithms to fine-grained word senses, senses that rarely occur in texts often cause problems, as these cases are difficult to detect without relying on hand-tagged data. This is why many WSD systems use sense-tagged corpora such as SemCor to discard or penalise low-frequency senses.

For our work, we did not want to rely on hand-tagged corpora, and we devised a method to detect low-frequency senses and to remove them before using our translation-based approach. The method is based on the hypothesis that word senses that have few close relatives (synonyms, hypernyms, and hyponyms) tend to have low frequency in corpora. We collected all the close relatives to the target senses, according to WordNet, and then removed all the senses that did not have a number of relatives above a given threshold. We used this method on nouns, as the WordNet hierarchy is more developed for them.

First, we observed the effect of sense removal in the SemCor corpus. For all the polysemous nouns, we applied different thresholds (4-10 relatives) and measured the percentage of senses and SemCor tokens that were removed. Our goal was to remove as many senses as we could, while keeping as many tokens as possible. Table 3 shows the results of the process on all 5,438 polysemous nouns in SemCor for a total of 18,912 senses and 70,238 tokens. The average number of senses per token initially is 3.47.

For the lowest threshold (4) we can see that we are able to remove a large number of senses from consideration (40%), keeping 85% of the tokens in SemCor. Higher thresholds can remove more senses, but it forces us to discard more valid tokens. In Table 3, the best ratios are given by lower thresholds, suggesting that conservative approaches would be better. However, we have to take into account that unsupervised state-of-the-art WSD methods on fine-grained senses perform below 50% recall on this dataset[10], and therefore an approach that is more aggressive may be worth trying.

We applied this heuristic method in our experiments and decided to measure the effect of the threshold parameter by relying on SemCor and the Senseval-3 training data. Thus, we tested the MT-based system for different threshold values, removing the senses for consideration when the relative number was below the threshold. The results of the experiments using this technique will be described in Section 5.3.

5.2 Baseline system

We performed experiments on Senseval-3 test data with both MT-based and dictionary-based approaches. We show the results for nouns and adjectives in Table 4, together with the MFS baseline (obtained from the Senseval-3 lexical sample training data). We can see that the results are similar for nouns, while for adjectives the MT-based system achieves significantly better recall. Overall, the performance was much lower than our previous 2-way disambiguation. The system also ranks below the MFS baseline.

One of the main reasons for the low performance was that senses with few examples in the test data are over-represented in training. This is because we trained the classifiers on equal number of maximumly 200 sense examples for every sense, no matter how rarely a sense actually occurs in real text. As we explained in the previous section, this problem could be alleviated for nouns by using the relative-based heuristics. We only implemented the MT-based approach for the rest of the experiments, as it performed better than the dictionary-based one.

5.3 Relative threshold

In this section we explored the contribution of the relative-based threshold to the system. We tested the system only on nouns. In order to tune the threshold parameter, we first applied the method on SemCor and the Senseval-3 training data. We used hand-tagged corpora from two different sources to see whether the method was generic enough to be applied on unseen test data. Note also that we used this experiment to define a general threshold for the heuristic, instead of optimising it for different words. Once the threshold is fixed, it will be used for all target words.

[10]Best score in Senseval-3 for nouns without SemCor or hand-tagged data: 47.5% recall (figure obtained from http://www.senseval.org).

Word	Test Ex.	MFS	Dictionary-based	MT-based
Nouns	1807	54.23	40.07	**40.73**
Adjs	159	49.69	15.74	**23.29**
Overall	1966	53.86	38.10	**39.32**

Table 4: Averaged recall(%) for the dictionary-based and MT-based methods in Senseval-3 lexical-sample data. The MFS baseline(%) and the number of testing examples are also shown.

Threshold	Avg. test ambiguity	Senseval-3	SemCor
0	5.80	40.68	30.11
4	3.60	40.15	32.99
5	3.32	39.43	32.82
6	2.76	40.53	34.18
7	2.52	43.89	35.94
8	2.36	46.90	39.15
9	2.08	45.37	38.98
10	1.88	**48.62**	46.16
11	1.80	48.59	**47.68**
12	1.68	48.34	43.63
13	1.40	47.23	45.31
14	1.28	44.32	42.05

Table 5: Average ambiguity and recall(%) for the relative-based threshold on Senseval-3 training data and SemCor (for nouns only). Best results shown in bold.

The results of the MT-based system applying threshold values from 4 to 14 are given in Table 5. We can see clearly that the algorithm benefits from the heuristic, specially when ambiguity is reduced to around 2 senses in average. Also observe that the contribution of the threshold is quite similar for SemCor and Senseval-3 training data. From this table, we chose 11 as threshold value for the test data, as it obtained the best performance on SemCor.

Thus, we performed a single run of the algorithm on the test data applying the chosen threshold. The performance for all nouns is given in Table 6. We can see that the recall has increased significantly, and is now closer to the MFS baseline, which is a very hard baseline for unsupervised systems (McCarthy et al., 2004). Still, the performance is significantly lower than the score achieved by supervised systems, which can reach above 72% recall (Mihalcea et al., 2004). Some of the reasons for the gap are the following:

- The acquisition process: problems can arise

Word	Test Ex.	MFS	Our System
argument	111	51.40	45.90
arm	133	82.00	85.70
atmosphere	81	66.70	35.80
audience	100	67.00	67.00
bank	132	67.40	67.40
degree	128	60.90	60.90
difference	114	40.40	40.40
difficulty	23	17.40	39.10
disc	100	38.00	27.00
image	74	36.50	17.60
interest	93	41.90	11.80
judgment	32	28.10	40.60
organization	56	73.20	19.60
paper	117	25.60	37.60
party	116	62.10	52.60
performance	87	26.40	26.40
plan	84	82.10	82.10
shelter	98	44.90	39.80
sort	96	65.60	65.60
source	32	65.60	65.60
Overall	1807	54.23	48.58

Table 6:Final results(%) for all nouns in Senseval-3 test data. Together with the number of test examples and MFS baseline(%).

from ambiguous Chinese words, and the acquired examples can contain noise generated by the MT software.

- Distribution of fine-grained senses: As we have seen, it is difficult to detect rare senses for unsupervised methods, while supervised systems can simply rely on frequency of senses.

- Lack of local context: Our system does not benefit from local bigrams and trigrams, which for supervised systems are one of the best sources of knowledge.

5.4 Comparison with Senseval-3 unsupervised systems

Finally, we compared the performance of our system with other unsupervised systems in the Senseval-3 lexical-sample competition. We evaluated these systems for nouns, using the outputs provided by the organisation[11], and focusing on the systems that are considered unsupervised. However, we noticed that most of these systems used the information of SemCor frequency, or even Senseval-3 examples in their models. Thus, we classified the systems depending on whether they used SemCor frequencies (Sc), Senseval-3 examples (S-3), or did not (Unsup.). This is an important distinction, as simply knowing the most frequent sense in hand-tagged data is a big advantage for unsupervised systems (applying the MFS heuristic for nouns in Senseval-3 would achieve 54.2% precision, and 53.0% recall when using SemCor). At this point, we would like to remark that, unlike other systems using Semcor, we have applied it to the minimum extent. Its only contribution has been to indirectly set the threshold for our general heuristic based on WordNet relatives. We are exploring better ways to integrate the relative information in the model.

[11]http://www.senseval.org

System	Type	Prec.	Recall
wsdiit	S-3	67.96	67.96
Cymfony	S-3	57.94	57.94
Prob0	S-3	55.01	54.13
clr04	Sc	48.86	48.75
upv-unige-CIAOSENSO	Sc	53.95	48.70
MT-based	**Unsup.**	**48.58**	**48.58**
duluth-senserelate	Unsup.	47.48	47.48
DFA-Unsup-LS	Sc	46.71	46.71
KUNLP.eng.ls	Sc	45.10	45.10
DLSI-UA-ls-eng-nosu.	Unsup.	20.01	16.05

Table 7:Comparison of unsupervised S3 systems for nouns (sorted by recall(%)). Our system given in bold.

The results of the Senseval-3 systems are given in Table 7. There are only 2 systems that do not require any hand-tagged data, and our method is able to improve both when using the relative-threshold. The best systems in Senseval-3 benefited from the training examples from the training data, particularly the top-scoring system, which is clearly supervised. The 2nd ranked system requires 10% of the training examples in Senseval-3 to map the clusters that it discovers automatically, and the 3rd simply applies the MFS heuristic.

The remaining systems introduce bias of the SemCor distribution in their models, which clearly helped their performance for each word. Our system is able to obtain a similar performance to the best of those systems without relying on hand-tagged data. We also evaluated the systems on the coarse-grained sense groups provided by the Senseval-3 organisers. The results in Table 8 show that our system is comparatively better on this coarse-grained disambiguation task.

6 Conclusions and Future Work

We automatically acquired English sense examples for WSD using large Chinese corpora and MT software. We compared our sense examples with those reported in previous work (Wang and Car-

System	Type	Prec.	Recall
wsdiit	S-3	75.3	75.3
Cymfony	S-3	66.6	66.6
Prob0	S-3	61.9	61.9
MT-based	**Unsup.**	**57.9**	**57.9**
clr04	Sc.	57.6	57.6
duluth-senserelate	Unsup.	56.1	56.1
KUNLP-eng-ls	Sc.	55.6	55.6
upv-unige-CIAOSENSO-	Sc.	61.3	55.3
DFA-Unsup-LS	Sc.	54.5	54.5
DLSI-UA-ls-eng-nosu.	Unsup.	27.6	27.6

Table 8:Coarse-grained evaluation of unsupervised S3 systems for nouns (sorted by recall(%)). Our system given in bold.

roll, 2005), by training a ML classifier on them and then testing the classifiers on both coarse-grained and fine-grained English gold standard datasets. On both datasets, our MT-based sense examples outperformed dictionary-based ones. In addition, evaluations show our unsupervised WSD system is competitive to the state-of-the-art supervised systems on binary disambiguation, and unsupervised systems on fine-grained disambiguation.

In the future, we would like to combine our approach with other systems based on automatic acquisition of sense examples that can provide local context (Agirre and Martinez, 2004b). The goal would be to construct a collection of examples automatically obtained from different sources and to apply ML algorithms on them. Each example would have a different weight depending on the acquisition method used.

Regarding the influence of sense distribution in the training data, we will explore the potential of using a weighting scheme on the "relative threshold" algorithm. Also, we would like to analyse if automatically obtained information on sense distribution (McCarthy et al., 2004) can improve WSD performance. We may also try other MT systems and possibly see if our WSD can in turn help MT, which can be viewed as a bootstrapping learning process. Another interesting direction is automatically selecting the most informative sense examples as training data for ML classifiers.

References

E. Agirre and D. Martinez. 2004a. The Basque Country University system: English and Basque tasks. In *Proceedings of the 3rd ACL workshop on the Evaluation of Systems for the Semantic Analysis of Text (SENSEVAL)*, Barcelona, Spain.

E. Agirre and D. Martinez. 2004b. Unsupervised wsd based on automatically retrieved examples: The importance of bias. In *Proceedings of the Conference on Empirical Methods in Natural Language Processing (EMNLP)*, Barcelona, Spain.

Y. S. Chan and H. T. Ng. 2005. Scaling up word sense disambiguation via parallel texts. In *Proceedings of the 20th National Conference on Artificial Intelligence (AAAI 2005)*, Pittsburgh, Pennsylvania, USA.

I. Dagan and A. Itai. 1994. Word sense disambiguation using a second language monolingual corpus. *Computational Linguistics*, 20(4):563–596.

M. Diab and P. Resnik. 2002. An unsupervised method for word sense tagging using parallel corpora. In *Proceedings of the* 40th *Anniversary Meeting of the Association for Computational Linguistics (ACL-02)*. Philadelphia, USA.

C. Fellbaum. 1998. *WordNet: An Electronic Lexical Database*. MIT Press.

W. A. Gale, K. W. Church, and D. Yarowsky. 1992. Using bilingual materials to develop word sense disambiguation methods. In *Proceedings of the International Conference on Theoretical and Methodological Issues in Machine Translation*, pages 101–112.

H. Li and C. Li. 2004. Word translation disambiguation using bilingual bootstrapping. *Computational Linguistics*, 20(4):563–596.

B. Magnini and G. Cavagliá. 2000. Integrating subject field codes into WordNet. In *Proceedings of the Second International LREC Conference*, Athens, Greece.

D. McCarthy, R. Koeling, J. Weeds, and J. Carroll. 2004. Finding Predominant Word Senses in Untagged Text. In *Proceedings of the 42nd Annual Meeting of the Association for Computational Linguistics (ACL)*, Barcelona, Spain.

R. Mihalcea, T. Chklovski, and Adam Killgariff. 2004. The Senseval-3 English lexical sample task. In *Proceedings of the 3rd ACL workshop on the Evaluation of Systems for the Semantic Analysis of Text (SENSEVAL)*, Barcelona, Spain.

R. Mihalcea. 2003. The role of non-ambiguous words in natural language disambiguation. In *Proceedings of the Conference on Recent Advances in Natural Language Processing, RANLP*.

G. A. Miller, C. Leacock, R. Tengi, and R. Bunker. 1993. A Semantic Concordance. In *Proceedings of the ARPA Human Language Technology Workshop*, pages 303–308, Princeton, NJ, March. distributed as *Human Language Technology* by San Mateo, CA: Morgan Kaufmann Publishers.

H. T. Ng, B. Wang, and Y. S. Chan. 2003. Exploiting parallel texts for word sense disambiguation: an empirical study. In *Proceedings of the 41st Annual Meeting of the Association for Computational Linguistics*.

G. Ngai and R. Florian. 2001. Transformation-based learning in the fast lane. *Proceedings of the Second Conference of the North American Chapter of the Association for Computational Linguistics, pages 40-47, Pittsburgh, PA, USA*.

T. Pedersen. 2001. A decision tree of bigrams is an accurate predictor of word sense. *Proceedings of the Second Meeting of the NAACL, Pittsburgh, PA*.

X. Wang and J. Carroll. 2005. Word sense disambiguation using sense examples automatically acquired from a second language. In *Proceedings of HLT/EMNLP*, Vancouver, Canada.

Projecting POS tags and syntactic dependencies from English and French to Polish in aligned corpora

Sylwia Ozdowska
ERSS - CNRS & Université Toulouse-le Mirail
Maison de la Recherche
5 allées Antonio Machado
F-31058 Toulouse Cedex 9
ozdowska@univ-tlse2.fr

Abstract

This paper presents the first step to project POS tags and dependencies from English and French to Polish in aligned corpora. Both the English and French parts of the corpus are analysed with a POS tagger and a robust parser. The English/Polish bi-text and the French/Polish bi-text are then aligned at the word level with the GIZA++ package. The intersection of IBM-4 Viterbi alignments for both translation directions is used to project the annotations from English and French to Polish. The results show that the precision of direct projection vary according to the type of induced annotations as well as the source language. Moreover, the performances are likely to be improved by defining regular conversion rules among POS tags and dependencies.

1 Introduction

A clear imbalance may be observed between languages, such as English or French, for which a number of NLP tools as well as different linguistic resources exist (Leech, 1997) and those for which they are sparse or even absent, such as Polish. One possible option to enrich resource-poor languages consists in taking advantage of resource-rich/resource-poor language aligned corpora to induce linguistic information for the resource-poor side from the resource-rich side (Yarowski et al., 2001; Borin, 2002; Hwa et al., 2002). For Polish, this has been made possible on account of its accessing to the European Union (EU) which has resulted in the construction of a large multilingual corpus of EU legislative texts and a growing interest for new Member States languages.

This paper presents a direct projection of various morpho-syntactic informations from English and French to Polish. First, a short survey of related works is made in order to motivate the issues addressed in this study. Then, the principle of annotation projection is explained and the framework of the experiment is decribed (corpus, POS tagging and parsing, word alignment). The results of applying the annotation projection principle from two different source languages are finally presented and discussed.

2 Background

Yarowski, Ngai and Wicentowski (2001) have used annotation projection from English in order to induce statistical NLP tools for instance for Chinese, Czech, Spanish and French. Different kinds of analysis were produced: POS tagging, noun phrase bracketing, named entity tagging and inflectional morphological analysis, and relied on to train statistical tools for each task. The authors report that training allows to overcome the problem of erroneous and incomplete word alignment thus improving the accuracy as compared to direct projection: 96% for core POS tags in French.

The study proposed by Hwa, Resnik, Weinberg and Kolak (2002) aims at quantifying the degree to which syntactic dependencies are preserved in English/Chinese aligned corpora. Syntactic relationships are projected to Chinese either directly or using elementary transformation rules which leads to 68% precision and about 66% recall.

Finally, Borin (2002) has tested the projection of major POS tags and associated grammatical informations (number, case, person, etc.) from

Swedish to German. 95% precision has been obtained for major POS tags[1] whereas associated grammatical informations have turned out not to be applicable across the studied languages. A rough comparison has been made between Swedish, German and additional languages (Polish, English and Finnish). It tends to show that it should be possible to derive indirect yet regular POS correspondences, at least across fairly similar languages.

The projection from French and English to Polish presented in this paper is basically a direct one. It concerns different linguistic informations: POS tags and associated grammatical information as well as syntactic dependencies. Regarding the works mentioned above, uneven results are expected depending on the type of annotations induced. This is the first point this study considers. The second one is to identify regularity in rendering some French or English POS tags or dependencies with some Polish ones. Finally, the idea is to test if the results vary significantly with respect to the source language used for the induction.

3 Projecting morpho-syntactic annotations

We take as the starting point of annotation projection the direct correspondence assumption as formulated in (Hwa et al., 2002): "for two sentences in parallel translation, the syntactic relationships in one language directly map the syntactic relationships in the other", and extend it to POS tags as well. The general principle of annotation projection in aligned corpora may be explained as follows:

> if two words *w1* and *w2* are translation equivalents within aligned sentences, the morpho-syntactic informations associated to *w1* are assigned to *w2*

In this study, the projected annotations are POS tags, with gender and number subcategories for nouns and adjectives, on one hand, and syntactic dependencies on the other hand.

Let us take the example of *Commission* and *Komisja*, respectively $w1_i$ and $w2_m$, two aligned words (figure 1). In accordance with the annotation projection principle, *Komisja* is first assigned the POS *N* (noun) as well as the information on its number, *sg* (singular), and gender *f* (feminine).

[1]Assessed on correct alignments.

Furthermore, the dependencies connecting $w1_i$ to other words $w1_j$ are examined. Foreach $w1_j$, if there is an alignment linking $w1_j$ and $w2_n$, the dependency identified between $w1_i$ and $w2_j$ is projected to $w2_m$ and $w2_n$. For example, the noun *Commission* ($w1_i$) is syntactically connected to the verb *adopte* ($w1_j$) through the subject relation and *adopte* is aligned to *przyjmuje* ($w2_n$). Therefore, it is possible to induce a dependency relation, namely a subject one, between *Komisja* ($w2_m$) and *przyjmuje* ($w2_n$)[2].

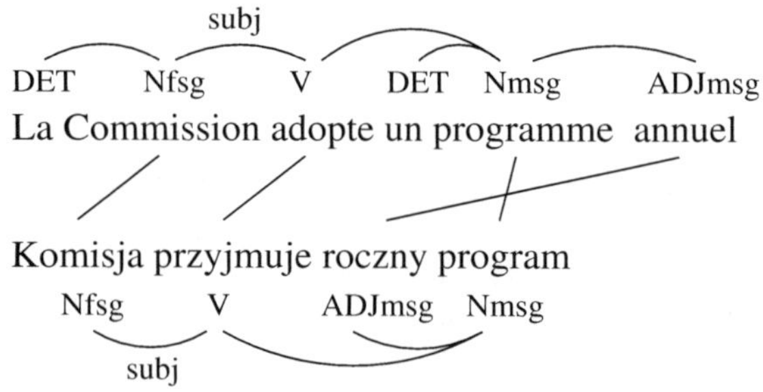

Figure 1: Projection of POS tags and dependencies from French to Polish

The induced dependencies are given the same label as the source dependencies that is to say that the noun *Komisja* and the verb *przyjmuje* are connected through the subject relation. Moreover, in this preliminary study, the projection is basically limited to cases where there is exactly one relation going from $w1_i$ and $w1_j$ on the one hand, and from $w2_m$ and $w2_n$ on the other hand. Thus, as shown in figure 2, the relation connecting *Komisja* and *przyjmuje* could not be induced from English since *Commission* and *adapt* are not linked directly but by means of the modal *shall*.

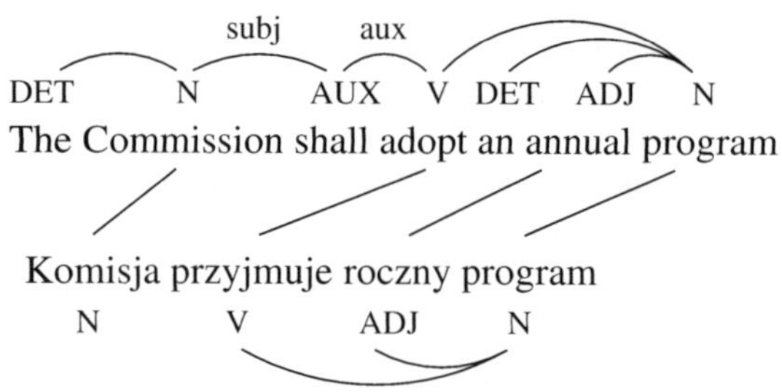

Figure 2: Projection of POS tags and dependencies from English to Polish

[2]The POS and the additional grammatical informations available are also projected from the verb *adopte* to *przyjmuje*.

The only exception concerns the complement and prepositional complement relations. Indeed, Polish is a highly inflected language which means that: 1) word order is less constrained than in French and English 2) syntactic relations between words are indicated by the case. This is the reason why, going back to figure 1, the projection from the nouns *programme* and *travail*, linked by the preposition *de*, results in the induction of a relation between the nouns *program* and *pracy*.

4 Experimental framework

4.1 Bi-texts

The countries wishing to join the EU have first to approve the *Acquis Communautaire*. The *Acquis communautaire* encompasses the core EU law, its resolutions and declarations as well as the common aims pursued since its creation in the 1950s. It comprises about 8,000 documents that have been translated and published by official institutions[3] thus ensuring a high quality of translation. Each language version of the *Acquis* is considered semantically equivalent to the others and legally binding. This collection of documents is made available on Europe's website[4].

The AC corpus is made of a part of the *Acquis* texts in 20 languages[5], and in particular the languages of the new Member States[6]. It has been collected and aligned at the sentence level by the Language Technology team at the *Joint Research Centre* working for the European Commision[7] (Erjavec et al., 2005; Pouliquen and Steinberger, 2005). It is one of the largest parallel corpus regarding its size[8] and the number of different languages it covers. A portion of the English, French and Polish parts form the multilingual parallel corpus selected for this study. Table 1 gives the main features of each part of the corpus.

	English	French	Polish
word forms	562,458	809,036	764,684
sentences		52,432	

Table 1: AC – the English/French/Polish parallel corpus

4.2 Bi-text processing

4.2.1 POS tagging

Both the English and French parts of the corpus have been POS tagged and parsed. The POS tagging has been performed using the TreeTagger (Schmidt, 1994). Among the morpho-syntactic informations provided by the TreeTagger's tagset, only the main distinctions are kept for further analysis: noun, verb, present participle, adjective, past participle, adverb, pronoun and conjunction (coordination and subordination). Nouns, adjectives and past participles are assigned data related to their number and gender and verbs are assigned information on voice, gender and form (infinitive or not), if available (table 2). The TreeTagger's output is given as input to the parser after a post-processing stage which modifies the tokenization. Some multi-word units are conflated (for example complex prepositions such as *in accordance with, as well as* for English, *conformément à, sous forme de* for French, adverbs like *in particular, at least, en particulier, au moins*, or even verbs *prendre en considération, avoir recours*).

4.2.2 Parsing

Each post-processed POS-tagged corpus is analysed with a deep and robust dependency parser: SYNTEX (Fabre and Bourigault, 2001; Bourigault et al., fothcoming). For each sentence, SYNTEX identifies syntactic relations between words such as subject (SUBJ), object (OBJ), prepositional modifier (PMOD), prepositional complement (PCOMP), modifier (MOD), etc. Both versions of the parser are being developed according to the same procedure and architecture. The outputs are quite homogeneous in both languages since the dependencies are identified and represented in the same way, thus allowing the comparision of annotations induced from either French or English. Table 2 gives some examples of the basic relations taken into account as well as the tags assigned to the syntactically connected words. The

[3]Only European Community legislation printed in the paper edition of the *Official Journal of the European Union* is deemed authentic.

[4]http://europa.eu.int/eur-lex/lex

[5]German, English, Danish, Spanish, Estonian, Finish, French, Greek, Hungarian, Italian, Latvian, Lithuanian, Maltese, Deutch, Polish, Portugese, Slovak, Slovene, Swedish and Czech.

[6]In 2004, the EU welcomed ten new Member States: Cyprus, Estonia, Hungary, Latvia, Lithuania, Malta, Poland, Czech Republic, Slovakia, Slovenia.

[7]http://www.jrc.cec.eu.int/langtech/index.html

[8]The number of word forms goes from 6 up to 13 million according to the language. The parts corresponding to the languages of the new Member States range from 6 up to 10 million word forms as compared to 10 up to 13 million for the languages of the "pre-enlargement" EU.

parts of speech are in upper case (*N* represents a noun, *V* a verb, etc.) and the grammatical information (number, gender) is in lower case (*sg* reprents the singular, *pl* the plural, *f* the feminine and *m* the masculine).

(the) Regulation_*Nsg* $\xleftarrow{\text{SUBJ}}$ establishes_*Vsg*
(le) règlement_*Nmsg* $\xleftarrow{\text{SUBJ}}$ détermine_*Vsg*

covering_*PPR* $\xrightarrow{\text{OBJ}}$ placing_*PPR* $\xrightarrow{\text{PMOD}}$ on_*PREP* $\xrightarrow{\text{PCOMP}}$ (the) market_*Nsg*
(qui) régissent_*Vpl* $\xrightarrow{\text{OBJ}}$ (la) mise_*Nfsg* $\xrightarrow{\text{PMOD}}$ sur_*PREP* $\xrightarrow{\text{PCOMP}}$ (le) marché_*Nmsg*

further_*ADJ* $\xleftarrow{\text{MOD}}$ calls_*Npl*
appels_*Nmpl* $\xrightarrow{\text{MOD}}$ supplémentaires_*ADJpl*
(the) Member_*Nsg* $\xleftarrow{\text{MOD}}$ States_*Npl*
(les) États_*Nmpl* $\xrightarrow{\text{MOD}}$ Membres_*Nmpl*
(the debates) clearly_*ADV* $\xleftarrow{\text{MOD}}$ illustrate_*Vpl*
(les débats) montrent_*Vpl* $\xrightarrow{\text{MOD}}$ clairement_*ADV*

(placing on) the_*DET* $\xleftarrow{\text{DET}}$ market_*Nsg*
la_*DET* $\xleftarrow{\text{DET}}$ mise (sur) le_*DET* $\xleftarrow{\text{DET}}$ marché_*Nmsg*

Table 2: Syntactic dependencies identified with SYNTEX

4.2.3 Word alignment

The English/Polish parts of the corpus on the one hand, and the French/Polish parts on the other hand, have been aligned at the word level using the GIZA++ package[9] (Och and Ney, 2003). GIZA++ consists of a set of statistical translation models of different complexity, namely the IBM ones (Brown et al., 1993). For both corpora, the tokenization resulting from the post-processing stage prior to parsing was used in the alignment process for the English and Polish parts in order to keep the same segmentation especially to facilitate manual annotation for evaluation purposes. Moreover, each word being assigned a lemma at the POS tagging stage, the sentences given as input to GIZA++ were lemmatized, as lemmatization has proven to boost statistical word alignment performances. On the Polish side, a rough tokenization using blanks and punctuation was realised; no lemmatization was performed. The IBM-4 model has been trained on each bi-text in both translation directions and the intersection of Viterbi alignments obtained has been used to project the morpho-syntactic annotations. In other words, our first goal was to test the extent to which the direct projection across English or French and Polish was accurate. Therefore, we relied only on one-to-one alignments, thus favouring precision to the detriment of recall for this preliminary study. Figure 3 shows an example of word alignment output. The intersection in both directions is represented with plain arrows; the dotted ones represent unidirectional alignments. It shows that the intersection results in an incomplete alignment which may differ depending on the pair of languages considered and the segmentation performed in each language[10].

[9]GIZA++ is available at http://www.jfoch.com/GIZA++.html.

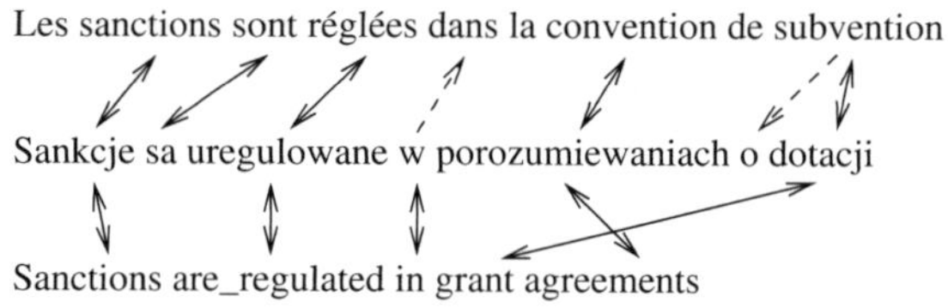

Figure 3: Intersection of IMB-4 model Viterbi alignments in both translation directions

5 Evaluation

5.1 Method

In order to evaluate the annotation projection, an *a posteriori* reference was constructed, which means that a sample of the output was selected randomly and annotated manually. There are some advantages to work with this kind of reference. First, it is less time-consuming than an *a apriori* reference built independently from the output obtained. Second, it allows to skip the cases for which it is difficult to decide whether they are correct or not: syntactic analysis may be ambiguous and translation often makes it difficult to determine which source unit corresponds to which target one (Och and Ney, 2003). A better level of confidence may thus be ensured with an *a posteriori* reference in comparison with a human annotation task where a choice is to be made for each case. Finally, whatever strategy is adopted, there is always a part of subjectivity in human annotation. Thus, the results may vary from one person to another. The major drawback of an *a posteriori* reference is that it allows to assess only precision

[10]The underscore indicates token conflation .

and not recall since it precisely only contains data provided as output of the algorihtm subjected to evaluation.

5.2 Parameters

The sample used in order to constitute the *a posteriori* reference is made of 50 French/Polish sentences and 50 English/Polish sentences. The same sentences in each language version were selected. Indeed, one of the goals of this study is to determine if the choice of the source language has an influence on annotation projection results. These 50 sentences correspond to 800 evaluated tags and 400 evaluated dependencies in the French/Polish bi-text, and 782 evaluated POS tags and 391 dependencies in the English/Polish bi-text.
Several parameters have been taken into account for each type of annotation projection by answering *yes* or *no* to the points listed below.
For POS tags:

1a. the projected POS is the correct one;

2a. the gender and number of nouns, adjectives and past participles are correct.

The gender parameter has been evaluated only for the projection from French to Polish as this information was not available in English.
For dependencies:

1b. there is a dependency relation between two given Polish words regardless of its label;

2b. the label of the dependency is correct.

Each time the answer to points 2a and 2b was *no*, the information about the correct annotation was added.

6 Results

6.1 Performances

Table 3 presents the number of projected POS tags and dependencies with respect to each source language. It gives the precision for each parameter, POS tag (1a), number and gender (2a), unlabeled dependencies (1b) and labeled dependencies (2b) assessed against the *a posteriori* reference.
It shows that the number of projected POS tags as well as syntactic relations is slightly lower when English is used as source language. A lower number of identified alignment links or dependencies may explain this difference. It also should be noted that the evaluated projections are not necessarily the same in both corpora. As mentioned in section 5.1, the same sentences were chosen for evaluation. Nevertheless, since word alignment depends on the pair of languages involved, it has an impact on the projections obtained and the *a posteriori* reference built on their basis.
The precision rates vary according to the type of informations induced. No significant difference is observed whether the source language is French or English. The number subcategory achieves the highest score: 0.88 and 0.91 respectively for French/Polish and English/Polish. Dependencies rank second—0.83 and 0.82—but an important decrease in accuracy—about 20%—is observed when their labels are taken into account. Finally, for French, the gender category achieves the lowest score: 0.59. The main reasons for which annotation projection fails are investigated hereafter. The projection of the number and gender subcategories are not taken into account.

		Fr/Pl	En/Pl
	projected POS tags	800	782
1a	*POS tags*	.87	.88
2a	*number*	.88	.91
2a	*gender*	.59	–
	projected dependencies	400	391
1b	*unlabeled dependencies*	.83	.82
2b	*labeled dependencies*	.62	.67

Table 3: Precision according to each evaluated parameter

6.2 Result analysis

There are various reasons for the failure of the POS tags and dependencies' projection: a) word alignment, b) lexical density, c) tokenization, d) POS tagging/parsing errors and e) insertion (for dependencies). In following examples, the word alignments are bold faced and in order to avoid confusion, the POS tags on the Polish side are the intended POS tags and not the induced POS tags.

a) The noun *countries* is aligned to *trzecich*[11] which is actually an adjective. On the other hand, *participation* and *udział* being aligned, the projected dependency is also erroneous.
***Participation**_N_1 of third **countries**_N_2*
***Udział**_N_1 państw **trzecich**_ADJ_2*

[11]The correct alignment is *państw*.

b) *Under* is translated by the prepositionnal phrase *na podstawie* but is aligned only to *podstawie* which is a noun. Thus, the projected tag cannot be assigned just to *podstawie*, which is also the case with the PMOD dependency between *zawarte* and *podstawie*.
***concluded**_PPA*$_1$ ***under**_PREP*$_2$ *the general framework*
***zawarte**_PPA*$_1$ *na **podstawie**_N*$_2$ *ogólnych ram*

c) This case is similar to the previous but the difference in lexical density is partly caused by the conflation of *in accordance with*, which corresponds to the prepositionnal phrase *zgodnie z*, at the post-processing stage of the POS tagging.
*They must be constituted **in_accordance_with**_PREP*$_1$ *the **law**_N*$_2$
*Muszą być ustanowione **zgodnie**_ADV*$_1$ *z **prawem**_N*$_2$

d) The following example shows an error in PCOMP attachement resulting in an error in dependency projection: *with* is linked to *pursue* instead of *activities* and the same relation is assigned to *o* and *zajmować*.
*They must **pursue**_V*$_1$ *activities **with**_PREP*$_2$ *a European dimension*
*Muszą **zajmować**_V*$_1$ *się działalnością **o**_PREP*$_2$ *europejskim wymiarze*

e) On the Polish side, the inserted noun *postanowień* governs *traktatu*. Thus, the PCOMP dependency does not link *dla* and *traktatu* but *dla* and *postanowień*.
*Without prejudice **for**_PREP*$_1$ *the **Treaty**_N*$_2$
*Bez uszczerbku **dla**_PREP*$_1$ *postanowień **Traktatu**_N*$_2$

Considering the precision figures, in particular those accounting for the projection of dependencies which decrease significantly when labels are considered, we tried to determine if there are indirect yet regular French/Polish and English/Polish correspondences. By indirect correspondence we mean that a given source POS tag or dependency is usually rendered by a given Polish POS tag or dependency. The correspondences are calculated provided there is no error prior to projection (word alignment, tagging or parsing).
Table 4 shows the direct and indirect correspondences among the POS tags which occur in the reference set. We can see that there is a direct correspondence among POS tags in 92% and 93% of the cases respectively for French/Polish and English/Polish projection. Moreover, the indirect correspondences, for example noun/adjective or verb/noun, are similar for both source languages. The following examples show occurrences of noun/adjective and verb/noun correspondences.

*the exercice of **implementing**_N powers*
*l'exercice des compétences d'**exécution**_N*
*wykonywania uprawnień **wykonawczych**_ADJ*

*measures planned to **ensure**_V dissemination*
*mesures prévues pour **assurer**_V la diffusion środki zaplanowane dla **zapewnienia**_N rozpowszechnienia*

Some indirect correspondences are more probable than others that seem unexpected. Most of the time the latter come from the differences in tokenization mentioned above.

Fr POS	**Pl POS**	**c**
N_359	***N_349**; ADJ_6; PPA_3;* V_1	.97
ADJ_74	***ADJ_69**; N_3; V_1; DET_1*	.93
V_68	***V_55**; N_13*	.80
PPA_67	***PPA_59**; V_6; ADJ_1; N_1*	.88
PREP_35	***PREP_24**; N_7; DET_2; V_1; PPR_1*	.68
others_61	same_**56**	.91
664	**612**	**.92**
En POS	**Pl POS**	**c**
N_374	***N_364**; ADJ_9; PPA_1*	.97
PREP_64	***PREP_53**; N_7; DET_4*	.83
V_51	***V_35**; PPA_10; N_6*	.69
ADJ_46	***ADJ_42**; N_2; V_1; DET_1*	.91
DET_36	***DET_33**; N_2*	.91
others_73	same_**70**	.95
644	**597**	**.93**

Table 4: French/Polish and English/Polish POS tag correspondences

Table 5 summarizes direct and indirect correspondences among syntactic dependency relations. It can be seen that direct correspondence rates for dependencies are lower than direct correspondences for POS tags: 78% when the source language is French source and 82% when it is

English. Moreover, the difference according to the source language—5% in favour of English—is more important than for POS tags—1% in favour of English. It is mainly due to the PMOD and PCOMP relations: the first connects a preposition to its governor and the second connects the dependent to a preposition. Since Polish is an inflected language, the connections between words are indicated through cases. In particular, it results in a noun not being necessarily linked to another noun by a preposition. This is also the case for English, as far as compounds are concerned, while in French a preposition is almost always required to form noun phrases. This is one of the reasons why the direct correspondence rate between English and Polish is higher than between French and Polish. The following example shows a direct MOD/MOD correspondence for the English/Polish pair and an indirect PMOD_PCOMP/MOD correspondence for the French/Polish one.

purity $\xrightarrow{\text{MOD}}$ ***criteria_N*** *substances_N listed*
les ***critères_N*** $\xrightarrow{\text{PMOD\_}\textit{de}\text{\_PCOMP}}$ ***pureté*** *des substances énumérés*
kryteria_N $\xrightarrow{\text{MOD}}$ ***czysztości_N*** *dla substancji wymienionych*

Fr DEP	**Pl DEP**	**c**
PMOD_111	**PMOD_56**; MOD_51; OBJ_4	.50
MOD_106	**MOD_106**	1
PCOMP_35	**PCOMP_25**; MOD_7; OBJ_2; PMOD_1;	.71
OBJ_23	**OBJ_16**; MOD_5; PMOD_2	.69
SUJ_19	**SUJ_18**; OBJ_1	.94
others_38	same_**38**	1
332	**259**	**.78**

En DEP	**Pl DEP**	**c**
MOD_95	**MOD_90**; PMOD_5	.94
PMOD_93	**PMOD_59**; MOD_26; PCOMP_4; OBJ_3; SUBJ_1	.63
PCOMP_64	**PCOMP_49**; MOD_8; PMOD_7	.76
DET_29	**DET_29**	1
OBJ_23	**OBJ_22**; PMOD_1	.95
others_18	same_**18**	1
322	**267**	**.83**

Table 5: French/Polish and English/Polish syntactic correspondences

7 Discussion

The results of the projection of POS tags and dependencies concur with those reported in the related works presented in section 2. First, concerning the number and gender subcategories, Borin (2002) has found that the former is applicable across languages whereas the latter is less relevant, at least for the German/Swedish language pair. As seen in section 3, the projection of the number subcategory offers the highest score and the projection of the gender the lowest—0.59. It was to be expected that gender would perform the worst considering its arbitrary nature at least in French and Polish. Indeed, there are three genders in Polish, masculine, feminine and neutral, as well as in English, and two in French. Thus, not only the number of genders across French and Polish is different but they are not distributed in the same way in both languages. The information on gender was not available for English, gender being assigned according to the human/non-human feature.

Considering POS tags, the level of direct correspondence is the highest one when compared to the number and gender subcategories as well as to dependencies. The precision performed is however lower with respect to the figures obtained by Borin (2002) on the one hand, and Yarowski et al.'s (2001) on the other hand. In Borin's study, precision was assessed provided the word alignments used to project POS tags were correct. In this study, precision has been evaluated regardless of possible errors prior to projection. When these errors are discarded, the precision rates are similar. In Yarowski et al.'s work (2001), the evaluation did not concern annotation projection but an induced tagger trained on 500K occurrences of automatically derived POS tag projections. Indeed, the authors claim that direct annotation projection is quite noisy. This study shows that such a simple approach can perform fairly well as far as precision is concerned. The results are likely to be improved by implementing basic POS tag conversion rules as suggested in (Borin, 2002).

For the projection of dependencies, defining such conversion rules seems necessary as suggested by the significant difference in precision when the projection of unlabeled and labeled dependencies are compared. Polish does not proceed in the same way to encode syntactic functions as compared to English or French. Nevertheless, some of the syntactic divergences observed seem regular enough to be used to derive indirect correspondences. Hwa et al. (2002) have noticed that applying elementary linguistic transformations considerably increases precision and recall when projecting syntactic relations, at least for the English/Chinese language pair. The present study suggests that this kind of approach is promising for the English/Polish and French/Polish pairs as well.

The exceptionnal status of the corpus certainly influences the quality of the results. Legislative texts of the EU in their different language versions are legally binding. Thus, they have to be as close as possible semantically and this constraint may favour the direct correspondences observed.

8 Conclusion

We have presented a simple yet promising method based on aligned corpora to induce linguistic annotations in Polish texts. POS tags and dependencies are directly projected to the Polish part of the corpus from the automatically annotated English or French part. As far as precision is concerned, the direct projection is fairly efficient for POS tags but appears to be too restrictive for dependencies. Nevetheless, the results are encouraging since they are likely to be improved by applying indirect correspondence rules. They validate the idea of the existence of direct or indirect yet regular correspondences on the English/Polish and French/Polish language pairs which has already been tested with some syntax-based alignment techniques (Ozdowska, 2004; Ozdowska and Claveau, 2005). The next step will consist in exploiting the indirect correspondences and the multiple sources of information provided by two different source languages. Moreover, using IBM-4 word alignments in one direction instead of the intersection will be considered.

This work mainly focusses on precision thus lacking information on recall. Larger scale evaluations would be necessary to validate the approach, particularly evaluations that could measure recall, since the amount of evaluation data used is this study could be considered too limited.

References

Lars Borin. 2002. Alignment and tagging. In Lars Borin, editor, *Parallel corpora, parallel worlds: selected papers from a symposium on parallel and comparable corpora at Uppsala University*, pages 207–217. Rodopi, Amsterdam/New York.

Didier Bourigault, Cécile Fabre, Cécile Frérot, Marie-Paule Jacques, and Sylwia Ozdowska. fothcoming. Acquisition et évaluation sur corpus de propriétés de sous-catégorisation syntaxique. *T.A.L (Traitement Automatique des Langues)*.

Peter F. Brown, Stephen. A. Della Pietra, Vincent J. Della Pietra, and Robert L. Mercer. 1993. The mathematics of statistical machine translation: parameter estimation. *Computational Linguistics*, 19(2):263–311.

Tomaž Erjavec, Camelia Ignat, Bruno Pouliquen, and Ralf Steinberger. 2005. Massive multilingual corpus compilation: Acquis communautaire and TOTALE. In *2nd Language and Technology Conference*.

Cécile Fabre and Didier Bourigault. 2001. Linguistic clues for corpus-based acquisition of lexical dependencies. In *Corpus Linguisitc Conference*.

Rebecca Hwa, Philip Resnik, Amy Weinberg, and Okan Kolak. 2002. Evaluating translational correspondence using annotation projection. In *40th Annual Conference of the Association for Computational Linguistics*.

Geoffrey Leech. 1997. Introducting corpus annotation. In Roger Garside, Geoffrey Leech, and Anthony McEnery, editors, *Corpus Annotation. Linguistic Information from Computer Text corpora*, pages 1–18. Longman, London/New York.

Franz Josef Och and Hermann Ney. 2003. A systematic comparison of various statisical alignment models. *Computational Linguistics*, 1(29):19–51.

Sylwia Ozdowska and Vincent Claveau. 2005. Alignement de mots par apprentissage de règles de propagation syntaxique en corpus de taille restreinte. In *Conférence sur le Traitement Automatique des Langues Naturelles*, pages 243–252.

Sylwia Ozdowska. 2004. Identifying correspondences between words: an approach based on a bilingual syntactic analysis of French/English parallel corpora. In *Multilingual Linguistic Resources Workshop of COLING'04*.

Bruno Pouliquen and Ralf Steinberger. 2005. The acquis communautaire corpus. In *JRC Enlargement and Integration Workshop*.

Helmut Schmidt. 1994. Probabilistic part-of-speech tagging using decision trees. In *1st International Conference on New Methods in Natural Language Processing*.

David Yarowski, Grace Ngai, and Richard Wicentowski. 2001. Inducing multilingual text analysis tools via robust projection across aligned corpora. In *1st Human Language Technology Conference*.

Association for Computational Linguistics
209 N. Eighth Street
Stroudsburg, Pennsylvania 18360